Leadership Skills for Peer Group Facilitators

Joan Sturkie
and
Charles Hanson Ph.D.

Resource Publications, Inc.
San Jose, California

Editorial director: Kenneth Guentert
Managing editor: Elizabeth J. Asborno
Cover design & production: Huey Lee

Reprint Department
Resource Publications, Inc.
160 E. Virginia Street #290
San Jose, CA 95112-5876

Library of Congress Cataloging in Publication Data
Sturkie, Joan, 1932-
      Leadership skills for peer group facilitators / Joan Sturkie
      and Charles Hanson.
            p.   cm.
      Includes bibliographical references.
      ISBN 0-89390-232-2
      Peer group counseling of students—United States. 2. Student
      counselors—Training of—United States. 3. Leadership. I.
Hanson, Charles, 1945-   . II. Title.
LB1027.5.S8533 1992   92-12103
371.4'044—dc20   CIP

96 95 94 93 92 | 5 4 3 2 1

To all the peer counseling teachers—past, present, and future.
With love, admiration, and respect.
—Joan

To my wife, Nancy, my daughter, Kristen, and my son, Eric.
They are my primary and most supportive group.
—Charles

Contents

Introduction   1

1. Peer Helping Groups   4

2. The Peer Helping Leader   11

3. Group Member Needs   17

4. Stages of Growth in a Peer Helping Group   27

5. Working with Group Process   53

6. Growth Factors in Groups   64

7. Building an Effective Working Group   96

8. Techniques and Skills of Group Leadership   115

9. What Do I Do When...?   127

10. Transferring from One Peer Helping Group to Another   142

11. Models of Peer Helping Groups   145

12. Helpful Reminders   150

Bibliography   156

Introduction

We learn from our peers. That's what peer helping is all about!

One summer, while conducting a peer counseling workshop at California State University at Northridge, we were told by a trainee/teacher who would be teaching her first peer helping class in the fall that she felt her main weakness was in group leadership skills. After the subject was covered in the limited time available in the training session, the woman felt reassured but also somewhat overwhelmed with all the information. When we asked how we could help her, she suggested that we write a book on group leadership skills. She felt it would be helpful to have something to take home to continue to study.

Several years have passed since that conversation, and many other people have expressed the same desire to have a book on group leadership skills specifically related to peer helping.

This book is written because of the requests of those people. Peers do listen to peers.

When a person agrees to teach a peer helping class, a great responsibility is undertaken, and a major part of that responsibility is to assume the guidance and direction (the facilitation) of the class.

1

While many men and women have been trained to teach a class, not many have been given instruction on group leadership skills. Therefore, they go into a peer helping class thinking they will teach it like any other class, but they soon find out that peer helping is different. The facilitators know they must seek new skills in order to be effective group leaders. This book is written to help people develop those new skills.

In order to address the concerns of readers who may be new to peer helping, Chapter 1 covers some basic issues. Experienced teachers may best begin in Chapter 2, where we discuss some of the qualities of a good peer helping leader. Chapter 3 presents three major interpersonal needs that students work to satisfy through participation in a peer helping class. These needs provide an understanding of personal issues, which emerge in a sequential process as a peer helping class develops.

Stages in the growth of a peer helping class are identified and discussed in Chapter 4. Chapter 5 presents leadership steps for working with the ongoing process of the class as a group. In Chapter 6 we identify several factors that account for what makes a peer helping class supportive, helpful and effective.

Chapter 7 describes the establishment of group norms and rules as important guidelines for the leader. Additional group leadership skills are presented in Chapter 8.

Sometimes peer helping teachers do not know how to handle certain situations which arise. Chapter 9 addresses ten of the most common questions asked by peer helping teachers. These questions begin with, "What do I do when...?"

Chapter 10 deals with the frustration felt by students when they transfer from one peer helping group to another. Chapter 11 presents different models of peer helping. The final chapter, Chapter 12, speaks directly to the teacher to give him or her helpful reminders pertaining to the role of a group leader.

This book is written so that a person may read it in its entirety, or individual chapters can be read as needed. Both authors are very familiar with peer helping classes and the demanding roles of teachers.

We hope that this book will make your job as a group leader easier and much more enjoyable. Your understanding and application of the ideas and techniques we present will make your leadership more effective— in building the class into an important support group for students, in making the class a more powerful learning environment, and in influencing the lives of students in positive and constructive ways.

Chapter 1

Peer Helping Groups

Recently, I (JS) conducted a peer helper training workshop for teachers/administrators/counselors/nurses who were looking forward to starting classes on their school campuses. I saw a wide range of preparedness and expertise in the individuals who were attending from many different school districts. Some had backgrounds in counseling; others had attended training seminars on the prevention of drug abuse, suicide, codependency, or date rape. However, some were coming with little or no idea about what happens in a group or what their role as the leader entails.

I particularly remember one young teacher (we will refer to her as Kristen) who shared with the group that she was three weeks into her very first year of teaching. Kristen was hired one month after school started to replace a teacher who suddenly resigned because her husband was transferred to another state. When Kristen stepped into the already existing classes, she found that her assignments on the high school campus included four periods of English and one period of peer helping. She felt confident in teaching English because it was her college major, and she had spent the past year in preparing herself to teach that subject. However, peer helping was a different story. Nowhere had Kristen received any training to teach the peer helping class, and the one teacher who knew about the class had just left to move across the country. Where could she find help to prepare her to meet a group of peer helpers each day?

Fortunately, Kristen was a bright, energetic, self-disciplined young lady who began to look for a place where she could receive training. She soon found that conducting a peer helping class is entirely different from standing in front of a lecture-type class. Successfully facilitating a group is a skill that must be acquired, and like the development of all other skills, practice is a necessary component.

Kristen was an eager learner, and after attending the workshop, she soon felt confident in leading her peer helping group. But what about all the other Kristens in the school systems who find themselves assigned to a class they haven't requested and know nothing about? Help must be available for them.

What is Peer Helping?

While peer helping has gained wide recognition and acceptance in the past decade, many people still do not understand exactly what a peer helping class is or what it does. What then exactly is peer helping? **Peer helping is a program where adolescents learn how to correctly and positively support one another.** One student defined peer helping as, "A class composed of trained, caring people who are willing to extend themselves to help others."

In order to understand how to lead a group of peer helping students, let us define the term "peer helper" for you. **A peer helper is a person who cares about others and takes time to listen to their problems and concerns.** Without giving advice, the peer helper assists the person in solving his or her own problem. By using helping communication skills (particularly active listening), the young person assists his or her peers in clarifying their feelings and looking for available solutions.

How Do I Get a Group Together?

Now that we know what a peer helping group is, the next question is, "How do I get a group like this together?" The answer to this question will depend on where you are. If you are in a school setting, the answer will be different than if you are in a church youth group or other adolescent organization in the community. However, there are some components which will be the same no matter where you are or what particular type of group you have. For example, having a cross-section of students is very important in all groups. If you are in a school setting, the ethnic makeup of your peer helping class should reflect that of the school campus. This helps students learn about cross-cultural diversity and trains them to be peer helpers to all the different groups on campus.

Not only do you want a wide diversity of ethnicity among students, but you also want to have students with varied academic abilities, attendance performances, personalities (e.g., both introverted and extroverted), social backgrounds, and levels of school participation. In other words, you do not want a class of all leaders; neither do you want a class of all nonleaders. You want some students who are strong emotionally and others who may come from dysfunctional families and are barely coping. All of these students can benefit from having a strong support group. Each person is valued as an individual, and personal differences are appreciated.

In peer helping, students learn how to help themselves as they are learning to help others. Students who enter peer helping benefit from having peers in class who listen to them. Having peers who are nonjudgmental is another plus. They do not have to worry about being put down in class because students know the importance of acceptance and being non-judgmental.

The Beginning Group

The beginning peer helping class consists of teaching skills such as active listening, sending effective messages, and decision making. There will also be units on building self-esteem, developing a helping relationship, and referring students to community resources. Students will learn by role-playing, listening to speakers, having lessons presented by you, and listening to each other.

Ideally, in the school setting, the peer helping class is taught on a daily basis as a regular elective class. Students receive credit for the course, and the grade is placed on the transcript. In schools where this is not possible, students may meet on a regular basis before or after school or during lunch. The same material is taught, but credit is usually not given. A cross-section of individuals in the group is still necessary. Leaders need the same skills to facilitate the group, regardless of whether they are meeting every day or just once a week.

The size of the beginning class may vary from eight to thirty-five students. You may want to start the first group with a small number of students until you become accustomed to dealing with group dynamics. However, you will need to realize that size is only one factor that influences how a group functions. Groups that are the same size may function very differently due to the composition of students and the leadership skills of the teacher.

Class size may be more important to some teachers than to others. It was very important to Mrs. Kincaid. Being a meticulous person, she felt most comfortable when everything was nicely tucked away in its own place. Because of her fear of having too many people in her class and disturbing the order of things, she never experimented with increasing the size of the group. Each time she started a new class, she would limit it to twelve people who met after school.

One day Mrs. Kincaid's class visited another peer helping group in a neighboring school district. She was amazed to see what happened in a class of thirty-five who met as a regularly scheduled elective class. A great range of life experiences were shared in this class. (The more people in the circle, the more likely it is that two people with similar life experiences will be able to relate to one another.) Mrs. Kincaid also noticed that the larger number of students were able to share the load of keeping the class going. In other words, students were involved in the group process, and the teacher did not have to carry the entire burden of running the group and "staying on top of things."

The next time Mrs. Kincaid started a peer helping group, it was a regularly scheduled elective class which met every day. She increased the size to twenty-five and the following year to thirty-five. However, the next year she went back to twenty-five. It did not take her long to realize that a larger group has its pluses, but it also has its minuses. Allowing each person to share his or her feelings took a great deal longer than it had in her smaller class. She also found that some students were able to "hide" in a larger class. In a smaller class, the spotlight can be more easily focused on twenty-five students, making it difficult for any student to hide. Mrs. Kincaid had little training in group dynamics, and she did not know how to "chain" or "connect" one student to another in order for that shy student to feel secure in a group situation. Teachers who feel more comfortable with one size group than another, may want to explore their own feelings and see if their lack of group training plays a part in their preference.

The goals of beginning peer helping are to train students in skills which will allow them to help other students solve their own problems and give them experience in interpersonal closeness. When this training is completed, students go on to the advanced class. Students are now ready to help peers who are not in the group. Prior to this time, students have been able to help only their peers in the group.

The Advanced Group

The advanced school-based class can meet daily as an elective class for training to continue. Students practice their skills as they learn about such issues as suicide, death and dying, codependency, AIDS, eating disorders, teen pregnancy, drug abuse, family problems, dating, and school problems. Emphasis is placed on supervision in the advanced class because peer helpers need to talk about the problems of the peers they are seeing. The peer helping group will be a support to these helpers as they "test the waters" with their new skills.

For both the students and the group leader, an advanced class is similar in some ways to the beginning class. Students sit in a circle, and activities and discussion are assigned to promote the same emotional closeness in the group. Group leaders continue to model facilitation skills. In one respect student demands on the leader may be less in that trained peer helpers are more responsible and capable of helping facilitate the group. On the other hand, student expectations may be greater because the students are more knowledgeable and require a greater degree of expertise from the leader.

Under supervision, students in the advanced group may also be trained to facilitate support groups on campus, so it is very important that you know how to model the correct way to lead a group. As a teacher, you may want to use this book to teach group leadership skills to the advanced peer helping class.

Chapter 2

The Peer Helping Leader

A leader can make or break a peer helping class. Good leaders normally have great groups, while ineffective leaders have complaining, closed, and negative classes. What then makes a good leader? Do they come from one group, such as counselors or psychologists? Can teachers be as effective? Is there a certain type of person who is the most successful? Let's take the first question.

What Makes a Good Leader?

We believe the first requirement is that **the group leader wants to be there.** Unfortunately, we have seen teachers who are given a peer helping class simply because the assignment makes the master schedule work out. A teacher has an unfilled period, and peer helping needs a teacher for that time slot. The teacher does not want to teach peer helping but is told by an administrator that there are no other options. Needless to say, this leads to an unsuccessful experience for the teacher as well as the students. Normally peer helping teachers have a real desire to teach the class, and their passion for their work shows. Students are indeed fortunate to be in these classes.

A good leader does not have a need to control but wants to empower students. For some teachers this will be a new concept. Teachers are accustomed to "being in control" in the classroom, and to give up some of this power may be difficult for them. Good peer helping teachers are like good chefs. The chef may put a mixture together, but it is the ingredients themselves that make the bread rise or the Jell-O congeal. The students in the peer helping class will make it rise and congeal, if the teacher will give them the power to make it happen.

A good leader genuinely likes and respects young people. This is something that cannot be faked. The kids will spot an impostor immediately. Along with this respect will come **a desire to truly make a difference in the lives of students,** and this is often done by giving them the opportunity to help each other. In other words, the teacher does the helping indirectly, and he or she feels comfortable with this. A good leader does not have a need to be in the spotlight or to have the class revolve around him or her.

An effective leader will be less directive in his or her teaching. He or she will not supply all the answers to questions and problems in class, but will encourage students to look to each other for solutions. Not only do students learn from this method, but they develop skills which will allow them to be independent and self-reliant when later problems arise and a teacher is unavailable.

Do Good Leaders Come from Only Certain Groups, such as Counselors and Psychologists? Can Teachers Be As Effective?

While psychologists and counselors are knowledgeable in counseling skills and often make excellent leaders, they are not the only ones who are capable of being effective. Good leaders come from many different groups. Teachers make excellent group leaders also. They need more initial training than counselors, particularly in counseling skills, but once they are trained, they can be just as effective.

One common mistake in selecting teachers is to think that just because they are excellent instructors in their own fields, they will automatically be good leaders in the peer helping class. We have seen excellent math, English, science, or history teachers turn out to be ineffective peer helping leaders. On the other hand, we have seen some teachers who were burned out and ready to give up teaching turn into wonderful peer helping leaders and, at the same time, find a new zest for teaching their other classes.

While leaders do not have to be counselors, psychologists, or social workers, the training and education they can receive definitely form a strong foundation for leading a peer helping group. In fact, many teachers discover their initial interest in counseling in a peer helping class, and later go on to become school counselors, psychologists, and social workers.

Is There a Certain Type of Person Who Is the Most Successful?

The main criteria for peer helping leaders is not what groups they belong to or what subjects they teach. The most successful group leaders will have qualities such as:

- a caring spirit
- a passion for the job
- an ability to be flexible
- a desire to keep confidentiality
- a genuine regard and respect for young people
- a respect from their colleagues
- a desire to continue learning and improving
- a willingness to empower students

Peer helping leaders need to take training themselves before they begin their job. Qualified peer helping trainers are available and often offer weekend courses. Even if a leader has knowledge of the skills required for teaching the course, it is important to learn some of the nuts and bolts from a person who has already taught a class and experienced some of the problems that may arise. It is also important to network with other peer helping leaders involved in the training in order to build resources for sharing materials, discussing problems, and getting support.

As soon as possible, you will want to become familiar with resources in your school and community. It is important that you have this information for your future use in teaching a unit on the subject and for knowing counselors, psychologists, and other mental health professionals to use as resources when you find yourself faced with a problem too difficult to handle.

Being a peer helping leader takes patience, understanding, and energy. It is not always an easy job. But it is very rewarding.

It doesn't take long before a leader is conscious of positive changes which are taking place in the lives of students. Effective peer helping leaders describe the group as, "The best class I teach all day." Or they may say, "This class is what has revitalized me and made me want to continue teaching" or "I'd give up any of my other classes before I'd give up this one."

Peer helping leaders typically find they receive much more than they give. Many have said they feel like they have learned as much as the students.

Several years ago, I (JS) trained a counselor from a neighboring school district to teach peer helping. Beverly was the right person for the job, and her classes were excellent. Word soon spread around the campus about her class, and students who got in felt fortunate because there was always a waiting list.

Recently, Beverly attended one of my workshops, and I was pleased to find that she was there to accompany her colleague, Ruth, who was in training to be the second peer helping teacher at her school. I was delighted when I found how Ruth was selected. It seems Beverly put a notice in the school bulletin stating that the administration had authorized her to interview a second teacher for peer helping. Anyone interested was to contact her in the next couple of days. Eight teachers applied to teach the after-school class.

Beverly stated that the teachers were all exceptional people, and her decision was so difficult, she solicited the help of another counselor. After Ruth was selected, the remaining seven asked if there was anything they could do to help on a volunteer basis. Beverly seized the opportunity and made them a part of a peer helping support group on campus.

How wonderful it was to hear Beverly's story because I realized that a good peer helping program will attract good teachers and counselors. Rather than having to search for the right person, gifted teachers are now volunteering to become a part of the class they know is making a difference in the lives of students—and in the lives of faculty, as well.

Chapter 3

Group Member Needs

Students entering a peer helping class bring basic
interpersonal needs they will seek to fulfill in relation to other group members:

- the need for belonging or inclusion
- the need to establish control in
  relationship to others
- the need for increased levels of openness

Meeting these needs is a natural process that occurs
when individuals are brought together in any group
(Schutz, 1966). Understanding the basic interpersonal
needs will help you in selecting appropriate activities
that facilitate need fulfillment for all members. Such
knowledge will also help you understand the behavior
of group members and know why that behavior
changes through the course of your class.

Inclusion

Inclusion involves becoming known by others and
feeling a part of the class. Through interaction, individuals express who they are and find acceptance from

others. Helping students talk about themselves and express their unique identity facilitates inclusion. Students who may be outgoing, popular, confident in themselves, or comfortable in being open with others are likely to find a sense of belonging easily and early in the class. Other students who may be quiet in initial meetings, more shy, anxious or uncertain are likely to take longer to experience this sense of inclusion in the class. Nevertheless, all students will seek some level of belonging. If that cannot be achieved in the class as a whole, individuals will find it through smaller subgroups or even in relation to one other person in the class.

Activities that organize individuals to talk and get to know each other can be helpful in promoting inclusion early in the class. This can be done in pairs or in small groups. Two-person interactions may work best for initial "getting to know you" activities and exercises. Learning how to introduce yourself and how to welcome a new person are useful activities. When pairing students in your class or organizing small groups, it is advisable to split friends into different pairs or groups. That puts everyone in the same position; that is, everybody will be talking with someone with whom they are not familiar.

Building pairs is a particularly helpful way to promote inclusion. Following this format, two people interact and spend a few minutes getting to know each other or talking about a suggested topic. Each pair then finds one other pair to form a four-person group. Introductions or discussion continues. Each person from a dyad introduces his or her partner to the other pair.

Instruction in communication skills early in your class will be important to building inclusion among members. Individuals can again practice skills in pairs. One person can function as the Discloser, talking about something personal. This could be a concern, a problem, an issue about which he or she has strong feelings, an idea or opinion about some topic, or just something he or she likes or dislikes. The other person can be the Listener, practicing the particular skill presented. Remember to change pairs frequently as a means for helping students to get to know all members of the class. Again, encourage students to avoid forming pairs with people they already know well.

Self-awareness activities facilitate a sense of belonging among members of the class. Learning how to tune in to feelings, how to recognize likes and dislikes and even personal hopes, dreams and expectations can promote self-identification. Inclusion is built by providing opportunities for students to express who they are amongst class members.

Perhaps some of the best activities for facilitating inclusion involve recognition of individual differences and similarities. Exercises, activities and discussion that help students to clarify their individual values or what's important to them can be particularly useful here. Helping students to hear, accept and respect differences based on race, culture, and family background promotes a strong sense of inclusion. And finding those interests, values, activities or ideas that they share similarly with others increases a sense of belonging.

The need for inclusion does not necessarily involve building close emotional attachments to others. It mainly includes self-expression, participation in the class, a recognition of some unique aspects of each person, and the opportunity for class members to get to know each other. Just being able to do these things will bring about a shared sense of belonging and inclusion among class members.

Control

The second interpersonal relations need for individuals involves asserting control. The common sense notion of control over others is typically negative. Most would naturally feel that attempts to control others for some personal goal, idea or gain is wrong. But control, as intended here, does not necessarily imply that kind of deliberate, self-centered manipulation in which one person gains at the expense of another. Whenever individuals are organized into groups, the need for control begins to operate. Control is often seen in efforts to influence others, to provide leadership for the group, to assist in making decisions, to help move the group along toward some agreed-upon goal. And such behavior is often constructive and positive in both intent and aim.

Control needs, nevertheless, can be expressed in ways that may appear negative or hurtful to others. Attempts to dominate the group or individuals in the group manifest control needs in a way that puts others down. Dominance here does not only mean the attempt to dominate through aggression. Talking loudly, criticizing others, name calling, rejecting, talking over someone else—all these are typically received as dominating in a negative, aggressive and/or destructive manner. Individuals also dominate in groups by constantly demanding to be the center of attention, always being the first to respond to questions presented by the teacher, or by attempting to be the most intellectual, the most comical, the most enlightened, or the most anything.

Efforts to assert control are negative when they result in someone feeling criticized, put down, ridiculed, rejected or otherwise hurt. Individuals who do this repeatedly are evidencing problems in asserting control needs. The need for control being expressed is not wrong or a problem in and of itself. But rather the way an individual or several individuals manifest it can be a problem. Therefore, someone who expresses control needs in a destructive manner can best be helped by acknowledging his or her need and then encouraging a more constructive and positive expression. Consider the following example:

RANDY (*in response to the question presented by the teacher, "Why do people use drugs?"*): I think using drugs is really stupid. People who do drugs walk around acting all weird and silly and that's dumb. All you're doing is frying your brain and creating bigger problems for yourself. I think they ought to put all druggies in jail and throw away the key.

LAURA (*in an angry tone*): I think you're stupid for thinking that way. People who've never done drugs shouldn't talk about what it is and what it isn't. You don't know what you're talking about.

TEACHER: It appears that both you and Randy feel strongly about this subject. But I'm concerned that the way you are attempting to influence each other is by putting each other down. Remember, our rule for the class is no put downs. I wonder if you could try another way to say how you feel about why people use drugs and maybe say something about what has made you feel this way? Randy, since you started, how about going first?

RANDY: Well, I just think its wrong to use drugs. And Laura's right. I never have used them 'cause if I did I'd really catch it from my parents. My dad's real strict and he'd bust me good if he ever caught me doing that. I guess I also get worried because I have a friend who's using more and more, and I'm afraid he's really changing because of it. And not for the better either. I don't mean to put you down, Laura. I guess I just worry about what drugs can do to you.

LAURA: You are right, Randy. Drugs are dangerous. But I think kids use drugs for a lot of reasons. Sometimes they're bored and just looking for some fun. And sometimes it just helps you relax and not be so worried all the time. Once you start and you hang around a group that does it all the time, it's hard to stop, even if you know it isn't good for you. I didn't like the way you (*to Randy*) said people who use drugs are stupid. I don't think that's true and it shows that you don't know how hard it can be stopping when everyone around you is doing it. At least that's how it's been for me.

TEACHER: Thank you for your comments. You both seem to have your own reasons and experiences to support your views, and I'm glad that you could express them in a way that helps us understand. Would anyone in the class like to respond to Randy or Laura?

In this example, the teacher points out the positive aspect of both Laura's and Randy's initial comments—they were both trying to express their strongly held views and to influence others in the class. The invitation to do this in a more positive manner leads to more personal disclosure as a means for expression and influence. Such influence here comes from the need to have some control over the discussion about drug use. To each individual, this is an important subject about which they have strong views based on background and experience. They both need to have their experience and background considered in any discussion in order to feel that their individual positions will be accepted and respected.

Consider also that few people genuinely change problematic behavior when they are forced or criticized. However, once their views and experiences are respected, they may feel comfortable enough to open up about a problem they would like to change.

Knowing that students need to assert control as a manner of expressing personal needs, feelings, or opinions should enable you to encourage rather than discourage such behavior. This knowledge should also encourage you to decrease your control of the class and give increasingly more control to your students. Control needs can be constructive both in their expression and their impact on your class. Your task as the leader is to facilitate the positive and constructive outplay of this need.

Openness

As in any relationship, once individuals feel they are accepted and belong in the relationship, and once they have established a sense of control through being respected for their ideas, needs and feelings, the need for openness arises. In other words, feeling a part of the class is necessary before individuals can move to address their control needs. Belonging needs are students' initial and early concerns. If these inclusion needs are effectively addressed and met in the class, then students will feel sufficiently comfortable to raise control issues. If these control needs are successfully resolved, the class will feel comfortable enough to deal with more personal needs for openness and intimacy. The need for closeness, as opposed to distance, in relationships is what characterizes the need for openness.

People have a need to be liked for who they are. This typically involves the need to be accepted and appreciated regardless of their views, feelings, or needs. People seek to find others with whom they can be comfortably open, with whom they feel validated and affirmed. They naturally want someone to care about them. They also want to feel emotionally close to others. Openness promotes this kind of emotional caring and closeness, and therefore it is something people need in relationship to others.

As your class progresses, you are likely to find that the need for emotional closeness becomes increasingly prominent. Students seek to talk about those matters that concern them most. They may open up about deeply intimate problems and issues. Others will respond with sincere expressions of interest and concern.

Students may spend time after class continuing to discuss issues brought up in class. Students may request more time for open discussions and less focus on structured or didactic learning. As topics such as family, drugs, death, loss, suicide, sexuality, eating disorders and others are raised, students will be eager to disclose their personal involvement with them.

It is not uncommon to feel uncomfortable when students raise deep personal problems and feelings. You may wonder if this is the sort of thing that should go on in a school classroom. Perhaps, you may think, such discussion would best take place in a counseling group. And if you don't have the skills of a trained counselor, you may even wonder if you're prepared to handle what students bring up. If you find yourself having these or similar thoughts, don't be dismayed. The fact that your class is seeking to fulfill their needs for openness is in itself an indication that your leadership has facilitated their working through other needs successfully to get to this point. And students know what they can handle.

We believe that the purpose of your peer helping class is to give students an opportunity to learn skills of helping and use them in assisting and supporting each other. So resist the temptation to discourage student openness and discussion of intense emotions. Make sure such feelings and issues have a place in your class, and encourage students to talk openly about their concerns. Trust that your students will be able to respond in a helpful manner to any student's concern. Students can and do care deeply for each other. This is what makes peer helping as powerful and helpful as it is.

Your knowledge of the needs students have in interpersonal relationships should help make your class the kind of environment where students can work through and successfully address these needs. You do this through your choice of exercises and activities that promote need fulfillment. You also do this by supporting and facilitating the kind of discussion that acknowledges student needs, particularly when those are needs for control and influence. In addition, you do this by allowing your class to be a place where students can find emotional closeness and intimacy, where they can talk openly with their peers, and where discussion of personal issues, concerns and problems is not only allowed, but invited.

Chapter 4

Stages of Growth in a Peer Helping Group

A ll groups—whether classroom groups, therapy and counseling groups, community groups, or family groups—go through various stages of growth and development. Just as individuals grow through various stages in their development, so do groups. In essence, every group of individuals has a life of its own—and develops its own unique identity. As you probably know from experience, each class of students you teach can have its unique feeling, tone, process, comfort, difficulties, frustrations, cohesiveness, and history—its unique identity. This group development and identity is more important in peer helping classes than in other classes. In peer helping you expect the class to develop through various stages. Unlike your role in other classes, you as a leader help to focus the class on its particular stage of development in order to help the class grow as a group.

This chapter will outline the four common stages in group development:

- Stage One: Orientation
- Stage Two: Acceptance and Togetherness
- Stage Three: Dissolution and Conflict
- Stage Four: The Effective Working Group

Knowing these stages will help you to identify what is going on in the group at any particular time and to understand the importance of what is happening. With this understanding you can determine how best to lead the group to enhance the interactions and responses of individuals in meeting the group's developmental tasks. Teachers who are not familiar with the stages of group development may lead in ways that counteract what the group and individuals within it need to do and want to do in order to make their learning from each other effective and important. Knowing group development will enable you to make the class a better place for members to grow and learn and make the learning useful and important.

Stage One
Orientation: Getting to Know You

Individuals come to a peer helping class with a variety of needs, expectations, and fears. Some are excited to be in the class. They may have heard about it from a friend who was in it last semester who liked the class. Or perhaps the excited people are eager to learn about helping others and becoming peer helpers. Other students enter seemingly more resistant and fearful. They may be afraid of opening up to fellow students about their personal problems or concerns. Perhaps they've heard that this is what is expected. Perhaps their particular problems are too painful to share. Or perhaps they feel ashamed to disclose too much. Students also enter the class with their unique styles and personalities. Some have a strong need to be liked. Some are uncontrollably outgoing. Some are shy. Some are withdrawn. Some are skeptical. And some may even resent being there, but won't let it be known.

Regardless of the particular makeup of individuals, their needs and personalities, all students enter the class with a need to know what they are getting into. They want to know what will be expected of them and what the particular norms and rules of the class will be. At this time students are particularly observant of the teacher or group leader. Given the typical operation of school classes, they want you to take a strong leadership role and set the structure of activities for them. However, if you assert too much control or fail to get them talking, you will facilitate their dependence on you and block free and more spontaneous expression in the class. Students begin to make judgments about the kind of class this will be based on how you act as a leader. If you attend only to those students who are outgoing and talkative, they will know that you may choose favorites. If you talk or lecture a lot, they will know that you want control and will likely give it to you. If you are personable and up-front with your feelings and expectations, they will begin to think they can trust you. And conversely, if you are structured and distant, they will function similarly with you and others.

All students come with concerns about how they will be involved in the class. Inclusion needs are initially strong as students tacitly identify those they like and dislike in the group and make early judgments about whom they might trust and mistrust. If activities in the early meetings call on everyone in the class to talk and interact with each other (e.g., in small groups and/or the large class group), the norm will be set for high involvement of all members. Students who are more quiet and introverted may at this point feel nervous and fearful with such expectations, yet hopeful of finding more acceptance and involvement than in other classes. Students who are more naturally outgoing and extroverted will relish the invitation to talk freely and openly. They may even begin to dominate the group as their need for inclusion is high and verbal.

In the orientation stage of the class, it is important for you, as the group leader, to provide students with information about how the class will function. Let students know that the class will cover topics and issues that will be personally relevant to them. Give some examples so students won't sit in fearful curiosity. You can make your own list, but here are some possibilities: communication skills, how to make and lose friends, how to help someone talk about a problem, family problems or concerns, dating and sex, drug use and abuse, suicide, coping with loss and grief, knowing yourself and your values, accepting the differences between people, career interests, and self-esteem or how to like and care for yourself.

Presenting Format: How the Class Runs

In addition to informing students about the content or subject matter for the class, let them know the format of activities (i.e., how you will run the class). If you plan to do some didactic instruction or lecturing, let them know that will be part of the learning process.

It's best, however, to keep your lecturing to a minimum. Lecturing keeps the learning focused on you, and students will thereby tend to constantly look to you for information and direction. They will become dependent on your giving answers and will limit their role to asking questions. A strong leader-centered group will get you a lot of attention, but it will ultimately diminish the class as a group and the learning students can obtain from each other. Therefore, we recommend that you balance lecturing with lots of group activities. Be sure to include both small and large group activities as some students will feel intimated by the expectation of talking in the class group as a whole. Since most peer helping classes and curriculum are organized this way, it should be no problem to let students know that talking in small groups or in pairs will be an important part of the class. And don't forget to tell them that you expect them to learn from each other and value what they get from other class members.

Typical format for peer helping classes also includes talks by speakers from outside the class, films, group discussion, and perhaps open class meetings. The open class meeting provides an opportunity for students to talk about whatever they want. It's also a chance to talk at length about some issue or topic that was cut short in an earlier class session. Some students will be thrilled to know they can talk openly about topics of interest to them. Others will find this uncomfortable as it raises expectations of having to disclose personal information to the class. We think it is important to tell students that you hope they will become comfortable in talking about personal concerns or problems, but that there is no pressure to have to do so. Before any student (or adult for that matter) can feel comfortable in disclosing anything sensitive or deeply personal, there must be a feeling of safety and trust in the group. And safety and trust in a group takes some time to build. So it is acceptable to go slow and for students to take time to experience a sense of trust and safety with other group members. At the same time, you can tell the class that building safety and trust will require taking risks of opening up with each other. Encourage students to avoid just sitting back and waiting for it to happen.

Confidentiality: The Cardinal Rule

With an emphasis on establishing norms of safety and trust, it is critically important to talk to students about confidentiality. **Tell the students directly that confidentiality is the most important rule for the group and that you expect them to adhere to it.** This involves students keeping personal information confidential. Students must have the attitude that whatever is discussed or presented in the class is special and cannot be talked about outside the class—particularly with anyone who is not in the class. That is a fairly stern standard. Should someone outside the class ask about what takes place in the class, students are only obligated to give general information about what the class does.

What class members discuss outside relating to what has happened in the class also deserves consideration. A guideline to follow is that any discussion of something or someone which takes place outside the class carries the expectation that those in the discussion will bring back what they discuss to the class. In other words, if a student talks about something that happened in the class with another class member and shares his or her feelings or reactions, he or she is obligated to tell those feelings and reactions when the class meets next time. The reasons for this are:

- It is important for group members to hear the positive feelings and thoughts of other members. This builds group cohesiveness.

- Any class member deserves to hear negative feelings. To withhold them is unfair and destroys group cohesiveness.

- Talking about positive and negative feelings helps students learn how to accept each other, resolve conflict, and build cohesiveness.

- Unspoken negative feelings lead to cliques. Subgroups destroy cohesiveness.

As a group leader you are critically responsible for setting the rule of confidentiality and enforcing it. We recommend that you get a commitment from each class member that they will adhere to the confidentiality rule. Having each class member sign a written statement can be helpful in this regard. Also let students know in the early stages that breaking the confidentiality rule is grounds for being dismissed from the class. That may seem too harsh, but experience shows that when confidentiality is broken, trust and safety in the class are diminished, if not destroyed. Students clam up and fearfulness permeates the group. In that type of atmosphere, students will be more than reluctant to disclose anything personal. And rightfully so! When mistrust, fearfulness and intimidation prevail, your class can be ruined. It is important to let students know that you will not let this happen and that you will strictly enforce the confidentiality rule. Should you fail to set the rule firmly and enforce it, future peer helping classes will be similarly influenced and it may be some time before you get a class you enjoy, where students care for and respect each other, and where learning comes from mutual sharing. Guidelines for handling the breaking of confidentiality are presented in Chapter 9.

Rules, Norms, and Guidelines: Too Many Spoil the Soup

Other rules and guidelines can shape the orientation stage of your class as a group. In promoting safety in the group, an emphasis on openness, listening to, and accepting others is important. Typically, students do not "learn" the value of hearing and acceptance in their prior schooling, so the peer helping class becomes perhaps the first place where such attitudes and behaviors are practiced. Acceptance means allowing someone to be and express him or herself without negative judgment. One may not like what another says or does or may disagree. That's perfectly reasonable—and to be expected. The point is that one's dislike or disagreement should not come with some negative judgment that portrays another as "less than," inadequate, or shameful.

Presenting the guideline of acceptance and openness will help students identify this as a goal for the class. In the orientation stage, you present this to the group. It will take continual effort to emphasize this goal and work at achieving it. You won't be able to get it by merely asking for it. Group members achieve this through interaction and discussion, wherein negative judgments and their impact can be pointed out and discussed.

There may be other group rules or norms that you want to present in the early class sessions. However, be cautious of overwhelming the group with rules, norms and guidelines early on. The class will work at establishing its own rules and norms through interacting with each other. In fact, it is important that they have opportunity for doing this based on their experience in the group rather than have it dictated by you as the teacher/leader. So in the beginning stage, in the first or second class session, present a few overall guidelines and let the rest emerge as the class progresses.

It is natural for some students—perhaps many—to experience resistance to the group in this early stage. Students need to get oriented to each other and to your style and expectations. Some may address the anxiety this generates by jumping in feet-first with little thought for how others will respond. Others are more cautious and protective. It is important at this stage that you promote acceptance of students' individual styles and ways of being in the group—both those who jump in eagerly and those who sit back cautiously. Eventually, as individuals persist in their styles, the impact of those styles on others can be explored openly. Such discussion will hopefully generate additional guidelines for group member behavior. For example, the class might request that those who talk easily and freely work at helping more quiet and withdrawn members open up and participate more.

It is common to think that establishing rules and norms for a class involves first identifying the rules, reminding students about the rules, and then enforcing them. Rule identification usually amounts to the teacher telling students the rules. Reminders are given verbally and sometimes with a printed list at the front of the room for all to see. Verbal reminders are typical for most teachers, leading to roles of class policeman, prosecutor, jury and judge. Enforcing rules may involve pointing out what a student is doing wrong and possibly some consequence (e.g., a talk with the teacher after class, the dreaded phone call home, a one-way trip to the office, or detention).

The problem with such rule setting is that it is primarily negative in focus. It puts you in the position of an authority with standards to maintain. That can deter you from your important role of facilitating the group, supporting students, expressing empathy, and helping students learn from each other. Even if you feel you can handle being in such a position, your constant function as the authority and rule enforcer for the class leads students to pigeon-hole you in that role. They will look to you when someone acts out or when there's a problem. You have the final word, not them. And when they get that message, they can easily take the attitude that what they have to say is less important.

We encourage you to set rules and norms in a different way—in a way that builds on your role as a facilitator of the group rather than an authority. **Rather than *tell* students what the rules and norms will be for the group, facilitate students in defining rules and norms for themselves.** Do this by asking questions or focusing on a topic that gets them to think about the kind of rules and guidelines they may need. Here are some examples:

> "If you were to tell something about yourself that you considered personal, what kind of

assurances would you need to feel safe in the telling?"

"How do you feel about students arriving late to the class? How would you feel if the class was renewing a conversation on a sensitive subject from the day before?"

"Would you prefer to be in a class where everyone participated or where only a few held the group's attention? Why?"

"Let's talk about this issue of outgoing people having an easier time talking in class. Can you suggest some things they can do to get others involved? I wonder if someone who sees himself or herself as more quiet can speak first?"

By asking questions and focusing, you heighten students' thinking about group rules and norms, and you communicate to them that their thoughts and concerns about these matters are important and make a difference. Of course, once discussion has ensued, you need to guide the class to taking on rules or guidelines based on their discussion. Again, the main rule to establish early is confidentiality. Keep others to a minimum so the group doesn't get bogged down with this task. Rules and norms will be established throughout the class.

Another important skill in developing group norms and rules is to use acknowledgment and reinforcement extensively. You can easily establish a norm in a group without ever stating it directly to students. Just acknowledge and reinforce those students who function according to that norm or rule and you will get similar behavior from other students. For example, you could thank those students who arrive on time and want to get started. Make sure you give eye contact to specific students when you do this. As another example, you could comment favorably to a student who asks another student about his or her feelings or opinions on some subject. In addition to making this positive reinforcement, give a reason as to why it was good. For example,

> "Tracy, I really appreciated the question you asked Laurie. You seemed sensitive to what she was talking about and I think that question helped her to say more."

You could even extend this by asking Laurie about how she felt with Tracy's question.

If you use a statement like the above, don't follow it up with an injunction for everyone in the class to do the same:

> "...and that's the kind of responses I'd like to see from all of you in the class."

Such a statement can be demeaning and negate the effect of your reinforcement. Students are not always that eager to get teacher approval when it's too obvious. Other students see that as an immature attempt to get teacher attention (i.e., brown-nosing).

If a student is breaking a rule or acting in a way that you think is damaging to the class, it is tempting to deal with it directly by commenting to the student. Again, such a response makes you the authority and class watchdog. While this may be necessary in some in-stances, it is generally best to raise the behavior of the student for discussion by the whole class. Ask the stu-dent what he or she is trying to communicate or what need is being expressed. Then ask others their feelings about what the student said or did. Follow up by invit-ing students to suggest how they would prefer another to act in the group. This manner of rule setting estab-lishes a norm of students' giving direct feedback to each other. Direct feedback becomes critically important in later stages of the group.

Stage Two
Acceptance and Togetherness:
The Honeymoon Stage

Usually peer helping class members start off with positive expectations that are met through openness in the group, a different structure for the class, and inter-esting topics and discussions. You will see the enjoy-ment students feel in attending the class by their attendance, promptness and shared efforts at uphold-ing group rules. Some students may comment about how much they like the class. You may get positive comments about your role as the teacher that will make your day and send you home walking on air.

If you've done your work as a group leader, you've probably fostered a sense of trust and safety in the group. Some group members may have begun to open up about very sensitive and personal problems or is-sues. Group members may take sincere interest and concern with those who've risked to open up. There's a sense of togetherness in the class, and perhaps a feeling that this class is special. All of this points to an early form of cohesiveness that the class has attained.

Early cohesiveness is an important stage in the life of your class as a group. It represents the fact that safety and trust have been established to some degree. It is a sign that members are feeling accepted and part of the group. Many peer helping classes attempt this level of positive feeling in the group and never go further. Maintaining it becomes the norm. Any effort at breaking the good feelings the group has becomes suspect and met with animosity or irritation. It is natural for group members to want to keep a good thing going— and to fear it being lost. So acknowledging the level of growth at this point is important.

As the leader, an important role you play is to point out the positive feelings among members of the group. Your own positive feelings are important to express as well. Encourage students to comment about how they are feeling about the group. **Also encourage students to make direct comments to others about something they said or did.**

Sharing warm and positive feelings is something that most people find uncomfortable. We can perhaps accept such feelings in our intimate relationships, but most people even find that awkward. So learning how to share positive feelings—to both give and accept them—is an important individual skill and one that's important to the life of the group. **Openly reinforcing or acknowledging positive comments made by individual class members is an important task for you as group leader.** Thank students for what they say or add to the group. Do this even if what they add is disagreement. Connect the positive comments of members to reinforce their bonding to each other and seeing the mutuality of their good feelings. Also point out the safety and trust that group members have developed.

The good feelings students generate toward each other and the class are important to the overall success of the class. Groups where feelings of togetherness and acceptance are high tend to encourage people to open up more. Thereby, the outcome of such groups is more favorable and highly valued. The more one discloses about him or herself, the higher the degree of acceptance and validation—and the more highly the group is valued.

The cohesiveness students experience at stage two is an important basis for moving on to later stages of group development. The absence of cohesiveness and acceptance at stage two will make later stages risky and even damaging. **Stage two is a base of togetherness and acceptance that makes class members value the class as a group and brings motivation for dealing with subsequent issues and problems.**

You might ask how you are to respond to someone who is critical of the group at this stage if you are trying to invite positive feelings. It's best to accept negative comments openly. For example,

> "Jerry, I appreciate your taking the risk to tell the class how you don't like discussing drugs. It's important that each person feels comfortable when they don't want to talk about a particular topic."

> "Kathy, thanks for telling the class you are bored with this activity. It takes a risk to open

up with such feelings in the group. I wonder
if others are feeling this way?"

Anyone who may be critical of the group needs to feel
as if his or her criticism is also accepted. It is not necessary for everyone to feel the same. Giving acknowledgment to this by hearing and accepting negative
comments can help a student eventually feel more positive.

At the same time, it is important not to focus extensively on negative comments. You can give some attention through facilitating discussion of the negative
views, but the group may not be ready to work through
strong negative feelings early on. The tendency at this
point is typically to reject the person making the criticism or presenting a pessimistic point of view. That you
cannot allow. Nevertheless, the tendency for students
to feel irritated or disgusted with negative expressions
points to the importance of positive expressions about
the group. So accept critical or negative statements and
acknowledge the closeness others feel. Reinforce any
student who may be critical or negative for his or her
honesty and willingness to be open. You may also want
to encourage that student to find ways to find value in
the class as a group.

Stage Three
Dissolution and Conflict:
The Party's Over

Just as the bright sun of warm, cohesive feelings needs
to rise to give the class a sense of close togetherness, so

must it set and give rise to darker and more foreboding feelings of conflict. It's probably common for teachers of peer helping classes to view conflict as destructive of the group atmosphere in the class. Most people, including trained counselors and therapists, are uncomfortable with the intense feelings that conflict evokes. When irritation or anger is openly expressed in a class that has been predominantly warm and supportive, it can feel like the best part of the class might be lost, never to be recovered.

Conflict and its attending feelings are necessary to the growth of your class as a group. Conflict is necessary for individuals in the group if they are to learn important things about themselves. In fact, openly expressed anger, irritation, disagreement, annoyance, or dislike are all signs that your group is progressing. The fact that such feelings can be openly experienced and expressed means that students trust one another to take the risk of being vulnerable with each other. If you are too quick to shut such expression down or waltz over the underlying conflict, you risk the following:

- keeping the group from important learning
- blocking the group from deeper understanding
- standing in the way of the potential closeness class members can develop to each other
- promoting a pseudo or false intimacy in the class
- preventing more meaningful interaction in your class

43

We don't think these are the outcomes you desire for your class or your students. But to avoid them, you need to become knowledgeable about conflict and skilled in helping your class work through it.

Sources of Conflict

There are many potential sources of conflict in a peer helping class. You may notice one or more students who have marginally participated or seem critical of the process based on their non-verbal behavior. Facial expression may tell of discomfort, dislike, or negative judgment. Perhaps the attention given you or other students is never direct. A student may have an angry disposition that keeps him or her isolated from others. Such an individual may repeatedly act in a suspicious and angry manner and thereby manifest a protective style probably learned from distrustful family experiences.

Value differences are another potential source of conflict. Differences in lifestyle, religion, attitudes toward school, socioeconomic level, racial and ethnic background all become areas from which conflict can emerge. Subgrouping by students often evidences critical attitudes in such terms as "nerds," "jocks," "druggies," "long hairs," "skinheads" and others. Even differences in preference for music become potentially divisive.

Competition often becomes a source of conflict in a peer helping class. Students compete for teacher attention, recognition as being the smartest, the funniest, the coolest, the most caring, and even the least involved. Students who may be quick to criticize another for some reason may be showing competitive resentment. The student who criticizes another for being a "brown nose" or "teacher's pet" may actually be sensitive to those who seem to win teacher approval because he or she has strong needs for approval that are either unconscious or uncomfortable.

Students who fail to participate or live up to the norms of the group often become targets for resentment and anger. Such students may be perceived as hiding or critical of others. It is important, however, to watch for the group's tendency to scapegoat a student. **In scapegoating, one student is seen as the reason for all the group's problems or somehow becomes the focus when any problem or issue emerges.** Scapegoating is common in groups, but it is destructive to both the scapegoat and the group. In this manner, the class may avoid problems or other problem members. And one student who tends to invite a victim role avoids the challenge to be different.

Progression of Conflict

Regardless of how conflict originates, its progression is fairly common. Two or more individuals come to think that their ideas are right and the other(s) wrong. These views are held with equal conviction on all sides. Critical, rejecting, and demeaning attitudes develop, leading to the view that one side is good and the other bad. Communication then breaks down. The two parties stop listening to each other even though claims are made that they have. With further negative expressions, the two conflicting parties are likely to break off any contact and communication. The perception develops that no matter what the other says, it can't be trusted— even if the communication is helpful in resolving the conflict. There ensues an evident lack of empathy and acknowledgment of the other. Evidence contrary to one's perceptions are ignored or denied. In and out of the classroom, each side may attempt to garner support for his or her position, thereby furthering any distorted views, and the cost to the other in holding theirs. Without any assistance from you, the class leader, the situation is likely to fester and generate ongoing distrust and ill will. Insincere efforts to resolve the conflict usually don't work, and the class becomes inhospitable to any further positive interaction.

It seems when conflict progresses in this manner that all that you've worked for in the group has been lost. It's hard for students to come to class with their usual positive expectations. And you may feel burdened with trying to jumpstart the group after many weeks of helpful activity.

Working Through Conflict

It is important for you to keep in mind that conflict is an important and necessary stage of the group's development. While you may feel uncomfortable with what has taken place in your class, the fact is that you can welcome it as something the group needs to work through. **Conflict is an opportunity for growth and learning that cannot take place any other way.** So while you may be anxious about how to deal with it, you can also be excited about the eventual positive learning and resolution that you will facilitate.

One guideline for working with conflict is to try not to resolve or dismiss it quickly. The anger and resentment students may feel can take time to diminish and work through. You may need to suspend scheduled class activities and subject matter in order to provide enough time to process what has happened and work through the conflict successfully. **Your willingness and demand to work the issues through demonstrates to students the importance of learning from conflict and lets them know that you won't avoid it even though it is uncomfortable.** Your goal is to assist students with looking more deeply into themselves and the source of their anger. At the same time, you don't want to support any uncontrolled expression of hostility, as that produces no learning and is only destructive.

A goal to keep in mind while working through conflict is that of maintaining the cohesiveness of the group. Conflict threatens group cohesiveness. For that reason it is important to remind students that the group is special and important, that they must continue to value the class as a group, and that they need to learn to respect one another and continue talking openly to each other. Emphasize that communication is important and that everyone in the class needs to hear from the various parties in the conflict. Criticism, ridicule and rejection are to be avoided in favor of listening and understanding. Individuals in conflict need to learn to feel and express their anger yet hold respect toward the individual(s) who has been hurtful or offensive. Your hope is that through talking, being heard and hearing the other, the individuals in conflict will diminish the intensity of their feelings, accept that they are not entirely correct, and acknowledge ways they contributed to the conflict and the need to change themselves.

It is important to invite the expression of understanding of each side of the conflict from other members of the class. Finding out why one feels as he or she does is important, but knowing that he or she has been heard and understood by others is critical. And one student can understand another even though he or she doesn't agree. It can also be helpful for class members to understand why they support one or another member in the conflict. Friends typically support each other out of loyalty, even though they may disagree. Such individuals can be equally helpful in furthering the learning their friend in conflict has difficulty accepting. You can stress that this is an important role for friends and confidants to take in the class.

Exploration helps open up conflict to provide areas for further understanding. This you can promote by asking and seeking questions that will further exploration and understanding from the class. Here are some examples:

> "What is it specifically about _____'s behavior that you don't like? How would you like him or her to be different?"

> "What did you feel when _____ did/said _____? What did you intend by doing/saying what you did? What difference do you see between your actions/words and your intent? How might you make them more congruent or alike?"

> "Does this problem reflect other similar problems for you? Does _____ remind you of other people in your life?"

> "How do you usually react in situations like this one? How could you change that?"

The goal here is to understand why one reacts as he or she does, to understand the source of one's feelings and behavior in past or current relationships, and build understanding that can lead to acceptance and change.

The shift from experiencing to reflecting on that experience (see the self-reflective loop in Chapter 5) is important to working through conflict. You may need to ask individuals to try to move away from their feelings and try to understand what happened and why they acted as they did. Stress that class members need to learn to accept negative feedback and learn from it. As everybody knows, relationships always have conflict sometime, so learning to work with the feedback received from others will make people better partners, friends, roommates, lovers and siblings. When in conflict, people often tell each other important things about themselves that may be difficult to hear and accept. Nevertheless, such truths may only be presented through conflict.

The Value of Conflict Resolution

In working through conflict, your class will develop even closer, more intimate feelings with each other. It takes a good deal of effort for a person to work through a problem and acknowledge being wrong or needing to change. Doing that in the presence of understanding and accepting peers can be a profound experience. Students will learn that it is possible to be angry and/or hurt, to express it, and to learn and work through it. For many this is an invaluable lesson. Many students come from families where anger is unacceptable, fearful, or destructive. There can be no more valuable learning than to see that such feelings are important and not

49

destructive, but in fact helpful. Strong feelings tend to generate closeness. Indeed, by feeling as strongly as one does, a person acknowledges the personal importance of an issue and the importance the other individual plays regarding that issue. It is not uncommon, for example, for individuals to react strongly to others who display traits or behavior that they themselves exhibit and don't like hearing about.

Learning how to express negative feelings is an important outcome of working through conflict. Students will learn to fight fairly and gain strength in knowing how to do so. You may need to stress some rules in this regard. For example, it is not fair to speak for other people in a conflict situation (e.g., "Everybody in the class thinks the same about you.") Students will need to learn to make "I" messages and speak only for themselves.

It is also helpful to stress that individuals should avoid saying what they think the other is doing, or interpreting the other's behavior. In conflict situations, interpretations of the other are usually mistaken. Clarifying such distortions, however, is how the conflict gets resolved. It's best to stay with the behavior one shows (including spoken words) and say how it affects you or makes you feel.

Another important rule is to give each party a chance to be heard. Encouraging individuals in conflict to paraphrase or feedback what they hear from their "opponent" can also help further understanding. Also, tell students to avoid bringing up information from other contexts or other times to bolster their arguments. That only serves to induce guilt and is unfair. It also helps to stress that a person may do something they don't like, but that they don't have to reject him or her outright.

They can still value someone even though they don't like everything that person does.

By working through conflict, students gain confidence in themselves. Knowing others support and understand them brings self-affirmation. And knowing they can express negative feelings and learn from negative feedback brings personal strength. There will always be situations in life where they may be criticized or attacked. If they can handle that pressure and deal with it, they will benefit. And they'll learn how to work through their problems and grow from them. They cannot expect more.

Expect your class to feel closer when they've worked through conflict. It's hard to say just how much conflict is necessary for this to take place. For some classes, one major conflict is sufficient to build the cohesiveness that results from the working through process. For other classes, one successfully processed conflict provides the base for addressing more difficult conflicts that follow. You have to make decisions regarding just how much conflict the group can handle at any one time. Too much conflict can overwhelm the group. And not enough will retard its growth and development. Conflict presented too early in the group will prevent the cohesiveness required to work it through—and thereby be threatening and possibly destructive. Conflict addressed too late in your class term may open up too much to work through in limited time. So keep your intuitive finger on the conflict pulse of the group and assist the class in moving into and through this important stage in group development.

Stage Four
The Effective Working Group

As your class gains experience in maintaining cohesiveness by working through conflicts, eventually a renewed sense of confidence will emerge among class members. The primary concern of group members in the working stage of the class is to be open and find emotional closeness. Students come to realize that all feelings and issues can be addressed within the class and worked through constructively. Individual input from all members will be seen as important and valuable. Students will be encouraged and rewarded by each other for working on their problems or issues in the group. The ability for group members to accept feedback—even negative feedback—from each other will be evident. These are some of the characteristics of a class that has reached the stage of effective work.

Chapter 5

Working with Group Process

Teaching a class in peer helping can be different than teaching any other course. Not entirely different—you still need teaching skills for presenting information, leading activities and discussions, and managing the class. But a peer helping class can invite a different way of being the class leader/teacher.

In most academic classes, you are in charge. You set the rules; the class members adhere to them. You present information and tell students what to do. You monitor student performance. Then you evaluate them on what they've learned. Teachers are trained to be in charge. Typically, they learn to direct and focus discussion, to raise questions and provide answers. Whatever students have to say is usually filtered through or directed at the teacher. That style of leadership is called **structure-centered leadership**.

The teacher of a peer helping class is encouraged to be different. Instead of setting the rules, you suggest rules and have the class discuss them. They agree on which rules to use, which to change and which to discard. Instead of you the teacher monitoring what students do, you get them to monitor each other. Instead of you doing all the teaching, you provide opportunity for students to learn from each other. Certainly you must be directive at times. But your direction is ideally balanced with a facilitative orientation. You try to facilitate interactions between students. You facilitate a discussion. You get the students talking and let them go. You don't always give answers, but encourage students to respond to each other. You may present a structured activity, directing students to talk in small groups about a particular topic. But once you have done this, you then encourage students to look at how they talked with each other, how their discussion has had impact on each other, how they've addressed the topic, and how they could improve their discussion. Your focus is not so much directed at what students say, but rather at *how* they say it and what that may mean. This is called **process-centered leadership**. And it calls for a different orientation, a different attitude. It calls for you to be the kind of leader who takes pride in the ability to get the group to do all the work. It calls for you to be less in the spotlight and to turn the spotlight onto the students.

For most teachers, this style of leadership is foreign—and many find it difficult. It's easy to rely on skills you've learned and approach a peer helping class in the same way you would any other class. But if you do this, you will make a big mistake. Both you and the students will lose something of great value. You will lose the power of students helping, caring, supporting, and learning from each other.

To become a process-oriented leader, you need to understand what "process" is all about. Process refers to the nature of the relationship between individuals who are communicating with each other. Process-oriented leadership focuses on the *way* individuals talk and what that *way* might mean.

Process can be best understood when it is contrasted with the "content" of communication. Content refers to *what* two individuals or a group is talking about—the subject of the conversation. Take the following vignette for an example.

Sally and Yvonne are two classmates talking about their discomfort and apprehension around certain boys in the class. The girls are not close friends, but they mention a party they both attended last weekend and things the boys did that they didn't like. Initially, Sally opens the conversation and mentions her disappointment with the boys. Yvonne feels similarly, but doesn't say anything. She doesn't know Sally well, and since she has seen Sally go around with both of these boys, she is not sure just how to respond. She gives a brief yes and nods her head. When Sally begins to talk about the party and what she felt, Yvonne begins to feel more comfortable and loosen up. She then tells Sally about how her perceptions and feelings are the same. She goes even further to state that she still likes one of the guys and wishes he wouldn't act the way he does at parties. Sally is interested that Yvonne likes one of the boys and she smiles and giggles and opens her eyes wide as she asks questions about Yvonne's affection. Then Yvonne says something critical about the other boy. Sally's smile goes away, her body turns slightly away from Yvonne, and she begins to rub the fingers of one hand with the other hand. When she speaks, Sally defends the boy against Yvonne's criticism and her tone is less excited and strident. Yvonne seems to sense something about this and says something nice about the boy.

You might have guessed that Yvonne was initially uncertain about what to say to Sally when she started talking about the party and the boys. She may have felt anxious about getting close to Sally and opening up since she did not know her well. Also, she might have felt hesitant to say anything about the boys since she had seen Sally talking with them at the party. All of this is the process of the conversation. Yvonne shows through the tone of her voice, the lack of initial words spoken, and perhaps her body position that she feels this way.

What other aspects of conversational process do you pick up in the vignette? What are the process cues? What might they mean about how Sally and Yvonne are feeling toward each other?

If you detected that Sally was interested and a bit excited by Yvonne's expressed interest in one of the boys, you are correct. But when Yvonne says something critical about the other boy, Sally's non-verbal behavior, words (i.e., defending the boy), and voice tone tell you that she didn't like it. We might speculate that Sally likes the boy Yvonne criticized and doesn't like to hear negative things about him from Yvonne, even though she can say critical things about him herself. We don't know, but it's a possibility. If we were interested in the process and what it says about the feelings and relationship between Yvonne and Sally, we might comment about Sally turning away when Yvonne gave her criticism. We might ask Sally what she was feeling when

Yvonne said what she did. We could also ask Yvonne to comment on how she is feeling toward Sally as a result of this conversation. In other words, the focus of conversation becomes the conversation itself. A process-focused leader directs people to reflect upon how they interact with each other.

An important aspect of process-oriented leadership is to develop a "here and now" focus in the group. When Yvonne and Sally talk about their experiences at the party, that is a "there and then" focus. It's something that happened a while ago and in another setting. However, as they begin talking about their immediate feelings toward the two boys, and particularly as they begin to have feelings toward each other about what is being said, they shift to a here-and-now focus.

Your goal as a leader is to make here-and-now feelings a major focus of discussion in the group. Immediate feelings, thoughts and behaviors take precedence over what has happened in the past in students' lives outside the group. Immediate experiences also take precedence over what is currently going on in students' lives outside the group. It will help if you attempt to categorize the topics of conversation as being focused on past events outside the group, current events outside the group, and present happenings within the group.

Generally, stick to the guideline that whenever something is currently happening in the group, that becomes the focus of conversation. However, don't be overbearing in following the guideline. For example, if a student is talking about how difficult it is to live at home when her father is drinking and she gets tears in her eyes in telling the story and really looks like she's sharing the pain of this in her life, don't change the topic to what two other students are whispering about as she talks.

Allow the girl to finish, encourage other group members to respond by giving their here-and-now feelings and thoughts to what she said, and then after there is closure on this girl's sharing, address the two students who were whispering to find out what was going on for them. To get to the here-and-now of that, ask other students how they reacted to the two students whispering. How did it make them feel? What did they think of it?

The idea of one or more group members talking about a particular topic, then getting other members' reactions to what was said, and then looking back on how the topic was discussed and what that means is called a **self-reflective loop** (Yalom, 1985). Your task as the group leader is to open up the topic for other members to add their experiences and thoughts, encourage here-and-now reactions to what has been stated, and then guide the group to reflect on how they talked about it (i.e., examine the group's process).

Another vignette may further clarify this concept:

> Early in an open group session, James, a vociferous, strong, and intense upperclass student exclaims to the group in general and to Jennifer (a mild-mannered, good-natured student who incurs favor with the teacher, works hard and has high grades) in particular, that people who get good grades are just brownnosers and teacher's pets and that getting high grades is dumb. This provocative disclosure generates considerable comments from students who strongly agree and others who strongly disagree with the statement. Many other students

say nothing in response and appear apprehensive about what is being said.

James's statement and the ensuing discussion can be viewed strictly in terms of its content—an intellectual discussion about the merits and objections about working hard in school and establishing positive relationships with teachers. Some may argue that school is boring, teachers are uninteresting, that life for kids should be fun rather than work, or that hard work doesn't matter if teachers don't like you. Others may argue that working hard will pay off later, that good grades make one feel good about accomplishment, that one doesn't get good grades solely to earn teacher or parent favor, or that working hard and liking teachers doesn't mean you can't have fun. All that is the content of conversation.

A teacher might have difficulty with students complaining about school and criticizing hard-working students. A hard-working teacher might even take offense and offer his or her own opinions protecting the good students and criticizing the attackers for being unmotivated. That also is conversational content and only adds more material—although it's usually more heavily weighted material because it is given by the teacher. A discussion that only generates this type of argumentative content is likely to leave group members frustrated, angry, resentful at James for criticizing Jennifer, discouraged about the group, and possibly dreading the next open group session.

A strong, process-oriented group leader/teacher will address this topic differently. First, the teacher will not criticize or argue with students who may not like school or who may prefer not taking school seriously. The teacher will appreciate such expressions of feeling because that indicates the students feel open enough in the group and trusting of that openness to say what they really think and feel. Such a teacher might be thinking that this and other students who have negative attitudes toward school may have never discussed this in a classroom with a teacher present. And no one may have ever taken an interest in such students' feelings and concerns, tried to understand them, or accepted them for having such feelings. The process-oriented group leader encourages others to express similar feelings in order to promote an open and honest sharing in the group, to generate an atmosphere that encourages the expression of negative feeling, and to provide an opportunity for students to talk about their true feelings and concerns.

The process-centered group leader also considers the process of James's statement from several perspectives:

1. Why did James say this after Jennifer had asked a question about the exam coming up next week? Did he perhaps have some feelings about the exam? Did he anticipate failing? Did he despise Jennifer because she would be prepared?

2. What made James bring this up as a general statement to the group? Did he want to avoid attacking Jennifer directly? Is there something about James that he avoids direct communication when he is critical? In fact, James had made several critical comments in the class after someone had just spoken, but the comments always addressed the topic that person

brought up and not the person. Would other group members recall this and perhaps confront James about his style of taking abstract potshots at people? What would happen if James were made to confront Jennifer directly about what he said? Would he back down?

3. Why is James so critical of hard-working students who like teachers and school? Does he feel inadequate in school? Does he have to lift himself up in the eyes of others by putting down people who are not like him?

4. Why did James set himself up for attack by the group? In actuality, this was a familiar way for James to involve himself in the group. He was frequently picking arguments and fights with other students. What does this say about his general way of interacting? Is this his manner of interacting at home? In fact, the leader in this group recalled another student commenting about James's family having lots of problems and their fighting a lot. Is this the only way that James knows how to get involved in the group? Is this the only way he knows to interact with others—to pick fights and arguments? Is this how he keeps himself separate and apart from others, and alone in his world?

5. James' comments can also be considered in terms of the group itself. The group had been talking about relatively non-risky subjects. It was early in the school semester and the group

tended to stick to safe topics and avoid arguments. Was this the first attempt to open the group up to honest negative feelings? Were some members feeling a need to be more genuine and less nicey-nice to each other in order to talk about what was more meaningful to them? And perhaps the group through James was testing the teacher to see if she really meant that they could talk about whatever they wanted in open sessions. Could this be an effort to see if the teacher is strong enough to manage angry feelings and criticism in the group without resorting to control, rule setting, or criticism?

There are many ways to focus on the process of a group. Where you choose to direct the group is up to you. It may be best to focus on how negative feelings are expressed to another and what would be the best way to express those feelings. This would set a model for subsequent expressions of negative feelings in future meetings. Or you may choose to focus on a particular individual if that individual has had too little or too much involvement in the group. The group focus will be important if you have noticed the members being stuck in some particular mode (for example, if the group has been only nice and supportive and has avoided negative feedback or has been particularly hostile or threatening).

Process-oriented groups become very potent in the experience of their members. Through process focusing, group members learn to express and hear feelings, give and receive feedback, help and support each other, share openly about themselves, and find that others share similar experiences and problems. Such an experience is uncommon in the lives of most students. Once students realize the potential for learning and caring in such a group, they become excited about the group and eager to participate in its process.

Chapter 6

Growth Factors in Groups

W e know from experience that peer helping classes are effective in helping adolescents and younger children in many ways. The proliferation of peer helping, the testimonials from teachers, parents, school administrators and particularly students attest to the value of helping kids learn how to talk and interact with one another. Students have improved communication with parents, peers and family members; friendships have developed where none existed; children have decided against suicide; drug use has declined or stopped; performance in school has improved; school attendance has increased; students feel better about themselves. These are but a sample of the benefits of peer helping classes.

But what is it about these classes that makes them work? Is it the subject matter? The teachers? The students? Probably several factors account for the benefits students receive in peer helping classes. While we don't know specifically, research on groups highlights some factors we think are important to effective and beneficial peer helping classes. These factors include the following:

- Common bonds
- Group coheseiveness
- Emotional expression
- Positive expectation
- Help for help-givers
- Information sharing and skill building
- Interpersonal learning
- Reality and responsibility

Your knowledge of these factors will make a difference in how you conduct your class. Even if you already can develop a group with these factors present, knowing what makes your work effective will make you a stronger leader who can confidently facilitate the class.

Common Bonds

While people of all ages have a need for acceptance and approval, that need is intense for most adolescents and children. They are in the process of forming a solid sense of themselves—an identity. The early stages of this developmental process find young people looking to others to establish some acceptable sense of self. Being a part of a group, dressing in the appropriate manner, behaving in a way acceptable for the peer group are of utmost importance. When peer acceptance is achieved, it can boost one's self-esteem, generate deep relief, and literally bring joy to life.

With such strong needs, peer helping classes can be powerfully helpful by presenting opportunities for adolescents to discover commonalties through which they can form bonds of acceptance. Those feelings, thoughts and needs which we all experience carry the potential to connect us meaningfully to each other. Through such connections we find self-approval, self-love and acceptance of others.

Most school-age children as well as adults know what it is to feel self-doubt. Most of us also experience frightful feelings of inadequacy at one time or another. Loneliness and alienation are also common human feelings. The need to be liked by others, the desire to not be alone, the wish to be valued are universal in human experience. Some young people suffer constantly with these feelings. Others experience them periodically. Too frightened to let others know for fear of further rejection and alienation, they hold their pain inside and avoid letting this part of themselves be known by others. Yet the very pain and fear that separates us also becomes an important source for intimacy, closeness and profound acceptance. It is often a surprise when young people find they are not alone, that other peers experience the same things they do. Finding that even the most popular and well-liked kids on campus get anxious, have problems, and feel self-doubt is eye-opening. To discover that they are indeed very much alike in their needs and feelings is a very therapeutic knowing.

Peer helping classes enhance this help-giving process by providing activities and discussions where commonalties are emphasized. Those icebreaker activities you orchestrate early in the class are important tools for students not only to get to know each other, but also to build self-estem, acceptance of and sensitivity to others, and mutual approval through sharing common feelings, needs and experiences.

Talk about what it's like to meet and talk with some-one you don't know, or discuss what it's like to go to a party or social activity where you don't know anyone. In small groups, ask students to share their experiences of such events. Ask them to tell each other what would have helped them. Everyone can relate to the discom-fort such experiences generate. Similar discomfort will likely be a here-and-now experience for many students in the early weeks of the class. You can ask students to apply the suggestions for helping in one context (i.e., parties) to the current context of the class (i.e., fearful and withdrawn students). The discussion of what would have helped in those moments brings direction about how to help each other through their present discomfort.

Any activity or discussion that assists students in sharing what they have in common will build a strong, helpful, and supportive group. Having only a few stu-dents share such experiences in the class can be helpful, but nowhere near as powerful as everyone relating to similar feelings or needs. That's why it may help in the early stages to organize students in small groups where each has opportunity to talk openly with a few others. Mix the groups each session or periodically so accep-tance and common bonds can build with all class mem-bers.

Group Cohesiveness (Bonding)

All groups, both large and small (work groups, class-rooms, schools, counseling groups, communities), de-velop an identity. Cohesiveness is established when that identity carries with it a sense of members valuing the class as a group. Cohesiveness is the sense of "we-ness" members feel through interacting together. It is the bonding of members to each other and the group. It is the glue that sticks the group members together. Whatever attracts members to the group shapes its cohesiveness (Yalom, 1985).

Cohesiveness can be seen in group members making comments about absent members. They are missed because they're important to the group. Cohesiveness can also be seen in efforts to involve all members in the group. Everybody's input is considered important. It doesn't matter that members like everything about each other. In fact, strong cohesiveness develops when individual differences and disagreements are tolerated, accepted and especially valued. The diversity of opinions, ideas, lifestyles and viewpoints makes a group cohesive because the variety itself is unique and important to how the group functions. Attendance, participation, and attentiveness are further signs of the degree of cohesiveness in a group.

Group cohesiveness is perhaps the most powerful factor that makes a peer helping group effective in its aims. Without cohesiveness, a group becomes splintered, subgroups develop, individuals feel isolated and alienated and few will risk opening up or sharing important feelings and needs. In a cohesive group there is a sense of mutual support and caring. Members trust each other. The experience of trust, caring and support encourages members to share openly, to risk being known, and to open themselves to learning from each other.

Cohesiveness progresses through two major developmental stages over the course of a peer helping class. In its early forms, cohesiveness can be seen as a liking members have for the class. Members feel a sense of belonging and support in the class based on involvement that has encouraged participation and acceptance. Students may express warmth to each other, liking of the class, and appreciation to the teacher. Statements of valuing and liking typically outweigh criticisms or complaints. If any member is strongly critical or caustic to others, there will be a tendency to quickly deal with the issue and dispense with any bad feeling. For individuals who may fear conflict or rejection—and there will be many such students in the class—this early untested valuing for the group is very important to the trust that is necessary to work through the inevitable conflict and difficulties that later arise.

The second stage of cohesiveness involves a liking and valuing of the group because problems and conflict are acknowledged and successfully addressed. Most people are familiar with the kind of closeness that comes from working through disagreements or hurt feelings. Anger and hurt may be difficult to talk about. But when we do express such feelings and feel we have been heard, the acceptance we receive is very powerful. Greater still is the valuing we feel when the conflict raised by our feelings results in a change of behavior or a feeling of acceptance and appreciation for our having raised the issue. This kind of tested closeness produces a genuine sense of cohesiveness that can only come in this manner.

Another way in which deeper levels of cohesiveness develop is when a class member takes the risk to tell the group about a personal crisis or problem. Others provide support through understanding, acceptance, and perhaps a willingness to help. The caring that the group shows becomes helpful in and of itself. And the successful risk-taking of one member generates further openness of others both in sharing similar feelings and experiences and in telling about other personal crises and problems.

Through conflict and personal sharing, class members develop mutual respect and valuing. Being honest becomes more important than being liked. In fact, group members may acknowledge that they may not particularly agree with another or even always like another. But the commitment to hear each other out, to value what each person has to say, becomes more important than liking. Deep and important levels of cohesiveness develop through this weathering storms and being intimate. There has to be conflict and vulnerability for class members to reach this level of closeness.

Many peer helping teachers are uncomfortable with conflict. They may see it as counterproductive and even destructive to the class. It is perhaps all too common for peer helping classes to stress positive feelings, support and caring for others. This often occurs along with neglect, avoidance, or minimal attention to negative and conflicting feelings. Some leaders may even find deep levels of personal disclosure too difficult for the group or themselves to handle. While such fears and tendencies to avoid are often natural, they can stand in the way of the class developing and growing through conflict, hurt and angry feelings. It becomes important for any teacher of peer helping classes to be aware of his or her own tendencies to avoid or deny negative feelings and conflict. Once aware of any such tendency, try to prevent that personal fear from controlling your response to conflict or negative feeling in the group. Approach conflict and difficult feelings with interest, concern, and an openness to explore and learn. Expect that what will come from working through them will enhance the group, bring members close together, and establish a level of cohesiveness that takes the class from being a nice experience to a very powerful and valuable learning experience.

Techniques for Building Cohesiveness

Cohesiveness is so important to your class that it warrants our presenting techniques to facilitate its development here. **In building the first stage of cohesiveness, the leader needs to promote involvement and responsiveness of all members.** Activities that call for interaction in small groups or total group involvement will facilitate responsiveness. Model responsiveness yourself by talking to all students in the class. Reinforce students for interacting with each other. This can be done through your attending to what members have to say to one another. Drawing the class's attention to what two students are saying is another form of reinforcement. And any expression of appreciation or liking of how two students are interacting or responding to one another lets the whole class know that this is desirable behavior.

An important technique for building responsiveness, as well as other helpful conditions in groups, is **chaining** students together. In chaining, you link individuals with others in the group. For example, suppose you were to discuss in your class the topic of how people feel in their families. After six students talk about how they feel, you recall that two students talked about being the oldest child with younger siblings. You can chain these students together by saying: "Juan, you and Stacey seem to be in a similar situation as the oldest

71

children in your family. You both expressed frustration and irritation with all that is expected of you by both your parents and brothers and sisters." Stop here and ask them to respond to your chaining. Then you could chain in others by saying: "Who else in the class is the oldest child in your family? How do you feel similarly to Juan and Stacey?"

Identifying commonalties and mutual feelings enhances cohesiveness in early stages. Here's an example:

> "Alecia and Sam, you seem to have similar feelings about not wanting to go on to college after high school and needing a break from school. I wonder if you both could say more about that."

This is similar to chaining students who share similar experiences, views, or feelings. Expressing commonalties or shared feelings you have with another class member or the group as a whole is another useful step.

Since valuing of the group is an important facet of cohesiveness, **encourage valuing expressions from individual members.** You may express this yourself. You can ask how individuals in the class feel about any particular class session. Also encourage expressions of warmth, caring and acceptance. Reinforce such statements when they are made by expressing your liking or by just saying "Thank you." Ask questions that call for comments of appreciation from others in the class. Many teachers have found it useful to reserve a few minutes at the end of each class or group session for students to give thank-you's and other appreciative comments. This is an excellent way to build expressed valuing and cohesiveness in the group.

Initial cohesiveness may take several sessions to build. There's no rule of thumb for when to move on. However, you may need to limit expressions of criticism, rejection, or conflict in the early going. The group is likely to not have a cohesive base to handle the intense feelings that may be aroused with such expressions or issues early in its development. That doesn't mean you punish or otherwise come down hard on negative expressions, for it is still important to see them as valuable and honest contributions. But negative expressions early in the group may signal a lack of empathy or acceptance on the part of the giver for how such statements will be received. And that's the best way to intervene and still be accepting of criticism. Acknowledge the feeling being expressed so that the giver knows it was heard. Then ask how that person expects others will receive what was stated and what he/she intends by expressing it. If the issue cannot be readily resolved, express appreciation for the concern, and comment that the group perhaps might not be able to address the concern fully at this time.

To move the group into the second stage of cohesiveness, it is important for you to look for situations where early cohesiveness can be tested. Any situation involving commitment to the group can be a useful issue in this regard (e.g., lateness to class, interruptions, leaving early, absences, talking out of turn, dominating class time and attention). Invite class members to use the group or a selected time in the group to talk about personal problems or crises. If someone takes the risk to do this, consider setting up students to be available to each other outside of class for help and support.

Roleplaying outside-the-class conflict situations can move the group to raise genuine conflict issues within the class. Once conflict or deep personal issues have been raised, make sure you process these issues by getting as many students in the class as possible to respond to the issue. Have the class reflect on what the experience was like when it is over and comment on how they feel. You can repeat any of the techniques mentioned for early cohesiveness (e.g., modeling, reinforcing, chaining, asking questions) in working to build cohesiveness after an issue has been raised. Your role here is critical in bringing up issues that will direct interaction to deeper and more authentic levels of honesty and openness, where commitment and closeness can be tested, and where the group can come to value each other and the group for its ability to withstand the storms of conflict, controversy, and vulnerability. The closeness that develops from your efforts will truly establish a deep and meaningful cohesiveness in your class.

Emotional Expression

A unique aspect of peer helping is its focus on feelings and the importance given to students' emotional experience in the class. This makes peer helping particularly effective and helpful for students. There is perhaps no class at the high school level that primarily takes as its subject matter the experiences, feelings, perceptions and thoughts of students. The subjects presented and discussed in peer helping give meaning and direction to the growth of each student. Many students report that their learning to identify and express emotions was an important part of the experience in class. This is particularly the case when students have learned to express difficult feelings like anger, annoyance, resentment, hurt, sadness, pain, and fear.

To promote the expression of emotion, you as leader need to be aware of emotions students are experiencing. Draw attention to feelings by asking for students to disclose them. It helps to be keen in your perception of how students respond to your queries. Many times when leaders ask, "How do you feel about that?" the response that comes does not express feelings but rather thinking. Here's an example:

ANITA: I don't like what Bob said about girls needing guys to take the lead in male/female relationships. I think that most of the guys I know would be afraid if a woman were too forward or assertive in seeking a relationship with them. I think that scares them away or makes them think all the girl wants is sex. And I've even heard Bob put down girls who he thinks are too opinionated. So most of us girls just play passive to suit the guys. And I think Bob is uncomfortable with strong women.

TEACHER: Bob, how do you feel in reaction to what Anita said about you?

BOB: I think Anita has an attitude about guys. She's just angry when she doesn't get things her way. And that makes her think that guys have to dominate women.

Notice that in the example Bob does not respond to the question. He gives his analysis about Anita and why she said what she did, but he does not express his feelings about what she said about him. So the best response for this teacher would be to immediately address Bob and say:

> TEACHER: Bob, I don't think you answered my question. How did you *feel* when Anita said that you put down strong women and feel uncomfortable with them?

> BOB: Well, I felt attacked and it made me angry. I guess I felt hurt too because I like to think of myself as being one of the more liberated guys.

Your interest in students' feelings will lead to feelings being a primary focus in your class. Asking questions that lead to feeling expressions will initiate that focus. Reinforcing students for opening up with their feelings will ensure that the focus on feelings remains supported by the group. Expressing your own feelings will demonstrate their appropriate expression and further support open expression of emotions in class.

Positive Expectation

Important to any peer helping class or group is the anticipation that what will be learned will be personally meaningful and beneficial. It is important that you believe that what you provide in the class, the curriculum, and the interaction among members can make a difference in students' lives and education. You may feel this about your class, but it's important that your feelings and expectations for the class are expressed in such a way that students know it. Fortunately or unfortunately, students tend to live up to the expectations placed on them. The absence of positive and hopeful expectations will often be met by low or negative ones. So we encourage you to look at the expectations you put on individuals and the class as a whole. They can and will make a difference in how your class functions.

Positive expectations are critically important when it comes to dealing with personal crises, negative feelings, confrontation, and conflict. In the face of stressful events in your class, you may become frightened, vulnerable, or insecure. If you respond to such events by taking control, punishing, criticizing, or otherwise assuming an authoritarian stance, you are likely to tacitly communicate that you don't believe any good can come from what has been presented. While we don't advocate your abdication of responsibility as a teacher, we do encourage you to open up to troubling problems and issues in the group. Invite them with expectation that the discussion and working through of these issues will be a positive and growing experience for all. Positive expectation can even be expressed when you do not know how a problem or conflict will work out. You may be uncertain or insecure in it, but believing the group can work it through successfully will turn it in that direction.

Expectations are often expressed without words. A frown or other look of displeasure in response to what a student says will let all students know of disapproval. The student who is critical of the class may be a thorn in your hopeful side, but even a positive view—indeed, even an appreciation—of such openly expressed criticism will communicate an important message to everyone in the class. Students will know that openness is welcomed. Students will also know that you respect them for what they feel and think. They will feel free to open up in your presence and in front of other class-mates. They will come to know that whatever they have to contribute, whether positive or negative, is valued by you. If you offer this as a model, you teach everyone in the class how to give it to each other.

So when problems emerge, greet them with hopeful expectation that much will be learned in working on them. When complaints are muffled, invite their open expression so the risk to tell them can be known and acknowledged. When conflict emerges, demonstrate positive expectations for the benefits you know the group will reap by addressing it fully and openly. Positive expectation for the experiences in your class presents a strong and forward-moving basis for learning and growth.

Help for Help-Givers

When peer helping classes work well, they give much help and support to all class members.

One of the most important and valuable factors that makes peer helping effective is the fact that students help each other. Teenagers are typically more inclined to listen to the advice and suggestions of their peers. They are critically concerned with how they appear to their age-mates and how they can act so as to be more accepted and prized. The natural proclivity peers hold toward each other makes the focus on peer issues and communication easily interesting and helpful. For most students, the peer helping class will be their first opportunity to interact meaningfully with peers who are different. Students who may be shy and withdrawn can talk with popular students who may be part of the "in" crowd. White students get to talk with Black and other minority group students about similar life issues and concerns. High-achieving students get a chance to know what it may be like for someone who is not motivated or supported in his/her interests and needs. The mere fact of interacting positively with someone different than themselves can open your students to new understandings and deeper levels of acceptance, tolerance and appreciation.

Given the correct environment, students will naturally seek to help others. The opportunity to help, particularly when it is favorably received, provides the help giver with a sense of importance and value. Knowing that active listening and caring acceptance can make a difference in another's life is a very rewarding experience. It makes students feel good. They gain a sense of importance and value to others and, through that, feel their own living has meaning. For those who may have severe problems or who may exhibit a damaged self-image, helping another can boost self-esteem, provide a positive distraction from their own troubles, and provide experiential knowledge that they are not alone in the difficulties life poses. Little can match this powerful help that help-givers receive.

Your task is to build this growth-inducing factor in your class. You do this by providing opportunity for students to talk openly to each other. You support this by breaking up cliques when you form subgroups for activities and exercises. You foster mutual support by teaching about good and bad help-giving and emphasizing active listening rather than telling another the solution to his/her problem. Your acknowledging and reinforcing the care and help given by others will generate more of the same and make students feel good about what they offer. Your ability to avoid giving your own advice and resist being the center of help-giving for the class will go a long way toward empowering students to become the key help givers for each other.

This goes against the grain for some teachers. But it is crucially important for you to put the reins on your desire to show care and give help, and instead facilitate students to give that to each other. They will get much more in the process. Your reward will be in watching that happen and knowing you played the critical background role to bring it alive. Sometimes this requires deliberately stepping out of the role of rescuer, healer, caring mother, or nurturing helper. Giving up those roles that return such good feeling may not be easy, but that is precisely what you must do to enable your students to gain the benefits these roles return.

Information Sharing and Skill Building

A lot of valuable learning takes place through the giving of information in a peer helping class. Much of this information is presented through the curriculum. The importance of self-knowledge in terms of likes and dislikes, values and interests, needs and wants is addressed in most classes. Information, practice and feedback in building communication skills forms a basis for much interaction that follows. Social skills are presented and discussed. Didactic information also forms an important part of subject matter presented in such areas as drug use and abuse, pregnancy, dating, sexuality, suicide, death and dying, ethics, relationships with parents, family communication patterns, alcoholism, drunk driving, friendship, loss, career development and many others.

Your peer helping class is probably structured to encourage students to talk about personal problems and give suggestions to each other. This form of help-giving information can be valuable to peers, not only because new ideas emerge that haven't been tested, but because the information shows caring and concern. While we know such advice is an all-too-easy form of help, it is nevertheless, often sought after by teenagers. It's easier for teens to couch support and care in suggestions on how to deal with a problem. It takes time and learning for people to grasp the value of listening and being there as important forms of help in and of themselves. But supportive listening, being an ear for another's risk-taking openness, and showing a concerned presence are valuable forms of help. Making students aware of this will give them a sense of value and importance that does not require even words or insightful advice.

In addition to information presented through instruction or reading, students provide important data informally both in and outside the classroom. Feelings and opinions about particular topics, reactions to how another acts or talks, and responses to questions all provide important personal information that can be very helpful.

Information giving has long been a desirable form of help and instruction for people. We tend to be anxious and insecure in the face of things we know nothing or little about. The thought that a problem could be solved or a fear assuaged with the "right" information is potentially very relieving. Explanations that help to clarify the unknown bring comfort in understanding. The need for young people to know more about themselves, about others, and about how they can best get along and help each other is of immeasurable value in supporting their growth and development. The fearfulness that surrounds adolescence will surely be diminished through providing useful information and building new skills.

Social Skills

A continual source of learning and growth in a peer helping class focuses on interpersonal communication or social skills. Your class may be the only educational arena at school where students can:

- develop their awareness of themselves in relation to others

- gain sensitivity to the feelings and experiences of others

- learn to appreciate their own and others' cultural and familial background

- learn to communicate appropriately and effectively

- experience the intimacy of mutual disclosure and support

Since the majority of people's lives involves social interaction and communication with others, this learning is invaluable. It will benefit students in their social lives with friends, family members, girlfriends and boyfriends. It will develop students in their career lives, making them more effective interpersonally on the job and more attractive as job and educational candidates. Furthermore, the success and confidence in social skills that students obtain in peer helping heightens their self-worth. They grow to like themselves more when they know how to be likable with others. Your belief in the benefits of peer helping for students' social lives contributes to their expectation and involvement in the class. When students expect the class will help them learn how to be a better friend and person in the world, they will naturally be motivated to soak up all the learning they can. Students want to learn social skills; it's a primary focus in their lives.

The range of social skills students can learn is considerable. Some of the group leadership skills we present in Chapter 8 will be relevant to helping your students learn social skills. Here's a list of some communication and social skills we've found valuable for students:

- **Avoiding advice-giving:** the problems of telling people what to do, think or feel.

- **Managing interpersonal space:** allowing silence in conversation, not interrupting, and avoiding talking at the same time as another.

- **Self-disclosure:** the benefits of telling something about yourself that others don't know.

- **Carrying on a conversation.**

- **Asking someone for a date.**

- **Good vs. bad helping communication.**

- **Giving positive feedback:** telling things you like about another.

- **Communicating negative feedback:** telling things you don't like about another.

- **Conflict resolution:** how to argue fairly.

- **Identifying and expressing feelings.**

- **Accepting others' differences:** being tolerant of differences between people and non-judgmental in response to how they differ from you.

- **Communicating non-verbally:** knowing what your body says.

- **Empathic expression:** giving understanding of what another is experiencing.

Interpersonal Learning

Every student comes to your peer helping class with his or her own unique way of interacting with others. Good and bad habits of communicating picked up from home, from friends or from peers at school will become evident as your class progresses. Through self-observation and interaction with others, students become aware of important aspects of their interpersonal behavior. They come to know their strengths and weaknesses. They see the abilities and limitations of others and attempt to model that which they like. They learn about how they affect others, the kind of impression and impact they make. When others' responses are desirable, students gain affirmation in their behavior. On the other hand, when they may elicit unwanted responses in others, they hopefully have the opportunity to learn why the negative response occurred and gain understanding of how to change to elicit a more desirable reaction. All of this shapes powerful interpersonal learning that makes your peer helping class an experience of deep personal value.

One area in which students can develop important learning is in their interpersonal distortions. It's common for most people at some time or another to see others not truly as they are, but in terms of how they think they are. This is usually based on insufficient information about the person. And it's also due to people's tendency to see others in terms of some fantasy they hold about them. Prejudicial thinking and perceiving is a good example. If a white person tends to see all Black people as alike in some way, such stereotypic thinking will prevent that individual from seeing true differences between people from the same cultural and racial backgrounds. The same is true for students who view all high-achieving students critically, for example as nerds or brownnosers. Similarly interpersonal distortion occurs if the high achiever considers all long-haired students as unmotivated druggies.

It is important for you as the class leader to draw attention to and address any interpersonal distortion that may arise. Such distortions are frequently evident when an individual's reactions to another are very intense, out of proportion, or inconsistent with what may have transpired between the two individuals. The following interaction demonstrates interpersonal distortion.

SHELLY: I think we should mix up our small groups more often so we can get to know other kids in the class. Also, if everyone were required to talk about their views on dating, I think the rest of us wouldn't feel so uncomfortable telling about how we feel.

FRANCISCO (*Grimaces, makes a face, and mumbles under his breath.*)

TEACHER: (Paying attention to nonverbal behavior and noticing the face and mumble) Francisco, you seem to have a reaction to what Shelly just said. Please share it with us.

FRANCISCO (*with anger shown by a tight face and intense voice*): She's always telling everybody what to do and I hate it. We're doing fine in our small groups. Why do we have to change? And besides, not everybody wants to talk about dating.

TEACHER (*concerned that Shelly be able to give her reaction*): Shelly, how do you feel in response to what Francisco is saying?

SHELLY: Well, I don't think that I'm telling him that we have to mix up the small groups. I just thought it would be a good idea. And besides, you asked what suggestions we had for our next meeting. He doesn't have to get so angry about it.

TEACHER: Francisco, what is it about Shelly that makes you respond with such intensity and anger? You said that she's always telling everybody what to do and bossing people around.

FRANCISCO: Yeah, whenever you ask for suggestions about ways to change our meetings, she always jumps in and has got something to say. I'm sick of it. Why don't we ask some other people here what they think. She's just like my sister. Always giving her two cents and taking over.

TEACHER: So you see Shelly's responding to my questions as her being controlling. I also get the sense that you resent her because she does give her opinions and ideas and that reminds you of your sister who may do that without being asked. How might Shelly be different from your sister?

FRANCISCO: Well, she's always piping up with something to say, just like my sister. I guess I've got a lot of anger about that 'cause my sister generally gets her way. But Shelly does the same thing. And most of the time we do what Shelly wants.

TEACHER (*noticing Shelly fuming*): Shelly, you seem to have something to say. Could you talk directly to Francisco?

SHELLY: I do give my opinions and ideas, but no one else seems interested enough to say anything. If you disagree or want to do something different, why don't you say something?

TEACHER (*showing empathy to Shelly*): So you seem to get annoyed with being labeled bossy just because you give your ideas. And you also seem to tell him you feel open to what he has to say even if he disagrees with you.

SHELLY: That's right.

TEACHER: Francisco, what is your reaction to what Shelly is saying?

FRANCISCO: Well, I suppose I could state my opinions more often, but I often feel it's not okay if they go against hers.

TEACHER: I wonder if that's what you feel about your sister—that she doesn't really care what you think. And sometimes you think that Shelly feels similarly.

FRANCISCO: That may be. Still, I think Shelly could give other people a chance to get their ideas out before she jumps in.

TEACHER: How could she do that in a way that would make you feel that she were truly interested in what you had to say?

FRANCISCO: Well, I suppose she could ask. And maybe wait until others give their ideas. It would even help if she'd check out if people disagree with what she says.

TEACHER: Shelly, I wonder if what Francisco is saying might be helpful to you. Could you see yourself doing what he asks?

SHELLY: Sure. I don't want to be seen as bossy. But I know sometimes people see me this way. I guess I never ask if they agree with me or not, so then I never find out. Makes sense that I should ask for other people's opinions.

TEACHER: It seems that you both learned something here and have been helpful to each other. Francisco, it seems you see people who openly take the floor to say what they think as possibly not interested in you or your ideas. That's how you've learned to see your sister. So you don't say what you think, but just get angry. And Shelly, you seem to recognize that giving your opinions and ideas without checking out what others think or how they react may make you come off as bossy—something you don't want to be. So asking questions will help you come across as less controlling and genuinely interested in others. Thank you both for making the effort to work through this important issue.

Francisco distorts his original view of Shelly based on his relationship and experiences with his sister. The teacher assists in pointing out how Shelly is different in her behavior from what he thinks and then looks to help both parties understand the reason for the distortion. Such conflicts are likely to emerge later in the group's development. When they do, it will help you and the group to be alert to the possibility of interpersonal distortion.

Peer helping can become a rich ground for many aspects of interpersonal learning. Helping students learn about the impressions they make on others or how they come across to others can be helpful. Students appreciate it when they can learn something about themselves from the honest feedback of their peers.

Generally, neither young people nor adults risk giving feedback in peer relationships if it may be negative or hurtful. Nevertheless, most of us wish to know if there's something that we do that is a problem for others. We want to know if we exhibit behaviors that turn others off in some way. We want to know if some mannerism or habit annoys others. Also, learning about our style or the way we normally function in groups or with people is an important part of interpersonal learning. The outgoing, extroverted individual can be helped by knowing that his/her constant verbal expression can be seen as dominating and exclude others. Conversely, the quiet introvert will likely benefit from knowing that she/he may stymie a situation or confuse people by not giving verbal expression to thoughts and feelings. Developing your class into a safe forum for this to take place will bring out the kind of learning and growth your students would naturally like to make.

Interpersonal Learning Activity

Organize students into two groups, with one group forming an inner circle and the other an outer circle. Individuals in the inner circle sit opposite to and facing individuals in the outer circle. One person in the inner circle takes three minutes to tell the person sitting opposite in the outer circle something about the outer-circle person he/she *likes* and something he/she *would like that person to change*. The focus for change should be on a behavior which, once modified, will make the inner-circle person like the outer-circle person even more.

When three minutes are up, the outer-circle person gives the same feedback to the inner-circle person. It is best for the person getting feedback to not ask questions or limit questions to one or two clarifying ones.

When one pair is finished (after six total minutes), the inner circle rotates one position to the left (or right), and the exercise continues in like manner. If your class is small, each person in the inner circle will give feedback to each person in the outer circle.

Then you facilitate open discussion about feedback people repeatedly received and how individuals reacted to it. This format can be used to communicate first impressions people make. Or first impressions can be shared along with later impressions. Students can also give feedback on how they perceive others expressing particular feelings (e.g., warmth, caring, anger, sadness, etc.) in the group and things they would like to know about each other (particularly feelings).

This exercise will be threatening for some students. Therefore, it is best to do it later in the semester, when the group has established trust and strong cohesiveness. You may want to start with only positive feedback before venturing into dislikes, negative feedback, or requests for a change in behavior.

The opportunity to express and work through issues, concerns or conflicts where strong feeling exists provides valuable interpersonal learning. Many peer helpers talk about their most important experience in the class involving a time when individuals expressed strong emotions to others. Instead of such feelings being the end of communication, as is typical outside the class, the feelings were explored, the problem was opened up and talked through.

Sometimes the strong emotion involves positive feelings. I recall one such incident where a student who had been struggling with feeling alone and left out at school was afraid to open up to others for fear of further rejection. When he finally took the risk to tell a small group of students about his depression and aloneness, he was surprised to find that several students wanted to stay and continue to talk with him after class. The caring and concern of others was not something he ever thought he would get. For him, that was the most powerful experience in the peer helping class and one that changed the way he interacted with peers and turned around his self-perception.

The opportunity to express strong feelings and learn from them allows students to face feelings and situations that raise deep fears. Many fear they won't be able to handle it. Some fear that with intense feelings of anger or hurt, no good will come of it but only more hurt and anger. Many fear that their image will collapse, or they will lose respect from their peers. The fear of rejection is also common. When these feared catastrophes do not occur—when instead new and helpful learning takes place—students come to value the group for allowing the experience and appreciate the sincere effort of the group in making such experiences happen.

In summary, interpersonal learning provides a strong factor in making your peer helping class rewarding and effective. To facilitate its development, provide opportunities for students to learn skills in talking with and getting along with others. Also, give students a chance to express strong emotion, to work out their difficulties with others, and to learn from each other. In addition, set up activities and exercises in which students can give and receive feedback on how they come across to others and how they could change to improve their relationships. As a part of this, include giving both positive and negative feedback. Encourage risk taking and honesty. Facilitate students' natural interest in learning about how to be a good friend and how to have more meaningful relationships.

Reality and Responsibility

The final factor that accounts for the effectiveness of peer helping is its focus on accepting the realities of life and taking responsibility for how one deals with them. This may seem like an elusive condition, but students tend to find that talking about their life experiences in groups and discussing major life issues gives them a deeper understanding about living. Through talking about their individual concerns and problems and finding out that they are not alone, students come to understand that life isn't always fair and things don't necessarily turn out for the best just because they want them to. For many, the realization that other young people have problems just as bad or even worse than their own leads to a realization that there is suffering in life that most people cannot escape. Students come to appreciate the pain of others and learn to support each other in it. If your class addresses issues like suicide, death and dying, and loss, it's likely that you will promote an increased acceptance of the reality of living and encourage students to make serious and concerned choices in what they do.

Encouraging students to take responsibility for themselves is an important facet of connecting with the reality of living. You encourage this in your group by addressing students as individuals and asking them to speak as such. Watch for statements students make in which they speak for others (e.g., "We all feel uncomfortable with this subject"). When statements like this are made, you need to direct focus to the individual making them and help him/her take responsibility for the statement (e.g., "John, you are speaking for the group when you say everybody is uncomfortable. I hear that you are uncomfortable, but I'm not sure everyone in class feels that way"). You will promote responsibility when you stop students from talking for others in the class. Frequently, students will come to the rescue of their friends or classmates when they cannot express themselves well, or when they may be too emotionally upset to speak clearly. It's important to address such behaviors by noting the concern being expressed, but still asking individuals to speak for themselves and allowing others to do the same. Here's an example:

ALICE (*sobbing*): I...just..don't...know what I feel. It really—

JANE: I think Alice is trying to say that she didn't mean to attack or hurt Fran when she said that Fran was mean. She just doesn't want Fran to put her down behind her back.

TEACHER: Jane, you seem concerned with how Alice is feeling now and want to help her. But perhaps it would be best for you to tell her how you feel and let her speak for herself when she's ready.

Getting students to speak for themselves and be responsible for their own behavior in the group is a goal requiring continual work. This facilitates students' taking the risk to openly express themselves and draws attention to the ways they may use others to stay disconnected from your class.

Chapter 7

Building an Effective Working Group

Once you have organized a peer helping class, your task is to shape the class into a safe working environment where students can learn through interaction with each other. You work to establish a set of norms, rules and roles that guides the behavior of members. **Norms** are unwritten, unexpressed, or implicit guidelines for member behavior. **Rules** are guidelines that are expressed explicitly by you, the leader, or agreed upon explicitly by members. Group norms and rules support the operation of growth factors mentioned in the previous chapter. This chapter will identify group norms and rules and what you do to establish them.

Direct and Free Communication

An important norm for a supportive peer helping class involves the freedom to interact. This involves students knowing and exercising their options to do the following:

- raise questions

- challenge information presented

- express feelings

- talk to each other

- tell their reactions to the class and the teacher

- relate their experiences both in and outside the class.

In building the norm of free interaction among members, you encourage spontaneous expression.

Spontaneity of interaction must be contrasted with uncontrolled or unfocused interaction. Students typically have a lot to say to each other when they enter a classroom. Some of what they say may have little or nothing to do with the subject matter of the class or with building a supportive group atmosphere. Freedom of interaction does not mean that class members can talk about anything anytime they want. Comments should be directed toward the current subject being addressed and the general purpose of the class as a support group for sharing personal feelings and problems.

In other words, Andy's whispering to Charles that Sylvia likes him and telling what she said would not be appropriate free interaction. Nevertheless, how should this be addressed in the group? You could make a rule that side conversations are not allowed. You could reprimand Andy and Charles for talking and direct them to pay attention to the subject of the class. Or you could direct attention to Andy and Charles and ask what they are saying to see if they want to contribute to the group. Of course, their conversation is not one they would likely tell the whole class, so the upshot of your question would be their telling you that what they were talking about was private. Then, as free interaction is foremost, you lead the class in a discussion about what it's like to have private side conversations in a class when other subject matter is being discussed. Students may risk telling how they feel rejected or insulted or offended or discounted by such conversation. Then you seek information from Charles and Andy about how they are feeling in the group and how they feel in reaction to what others are saying about their side conversation. This demonstration of free interaction lets students know that while they may engage freely in discussion, any talk can become a focus for attention and further discussion. This includes sharing feelings, giving feedback, and learning to be sensitive to other's feelings.

Through the process of discussing the impact of side conversations on the class, students engage in fulfilling the norm of free interaction and likely develop a guideline or rule for listening to others and attending to topics being addressed in the class. So students participate in the establishment of rules and norms in the class rather than have them dictated and enforced by the teacher.

The direction and focus of communication in your class is important in determining whether interaction is "free" or not. It is common in many classrooms for communication to go from the teacher out to the class and then return from individual class members to the teacher. In this interactional pattern, the teacher is like the hub of a communication wheel. All communication goes through her/him. Teacher-centered interaction is not free interaction. It demonstrates a dependency that both students and the teacher have on each other. The dependency could be due to a teacher's need to control the class, a need for dominance, an overextended style of extroversion, or students' dependency on the teacher for approval, acceptance, and control. Ideally, the interactional pattern in your class will look more like a complicated web wherein the center is miniscule or absent. **The pattern should demonstrate students freely communicating to one another.**

Your role in building the norm of free interaction is to facilitate and increase student-to-student communication. You do this by directing students to talk directly to each other. Here's an example:

DELORES (*facing and looking at the teacher*): I have a problem with the guys in class telling the girls how it should be and what they should do when we talk about this dating stuff. I wish they would listen to what us girls have to say sometime.

TEACHER (*looking at Delores*): Delores, I notice you're looking at me when you make that comment, but I gather that you are commenting about some and maybe all of the boys in the class. I wonder if you could look at those boys and tell them directly how you feel about their telling you how they think it should be.

DELORES: Well, okay. Mike, Ted and Andy are the main ones. (*Looking directly at each one.*) You guys are always telling the girls how you think we should be on dates and I resent it. I have feelings too and would like to have a chance to say how I feel without you guys trying to talk louder or making fun of it. That makes me mad and I guess it hurts too.

MIKE (*looking at the teacher*): I think she doesn't like it when the guys express their opinions about dating. Most of the time the girls like to have it their way. We've got to make the calls and pay for everything and treat them like they're queens and if we want to change the rules, then they get all heated up about it.

TEACHER: Mike, how about saying how you feel directly to Delores rather than telling me. It seems like you're reacting to something she said to you. I also sense that you feel somewhat like her when you say your opinions don't get considered, but you're just expected to be a certain way on dates. Could you tell her your reaction to her being hurt by not being considered, and then tell her how you feel about your not being considered?

MIKE: Yeah, Delores (*looking at her*), I think you just don't like it if we object to how you think dating should be.

TEACHER: Mike, tell Delores *how you feel* when what you want on a date is not considered.

MIKE (*to Delores*): Well, it gets me angry that as a guy whenever I ask a girl out I'm just automatically expected to pay for the date. And you just get angry when I or any other guy here expresses how they feel about that. I think we have a right to have our feelings considered too.

TEACHER: Thanks Mike, I wonder if you could tell Delores how you feel about her feeling neglected on this subject as well.

MIKE (*looking at the teacher*): Well, I'm—

TEACHER: Tell Delores, Mike.

MIKE (*looking at Delores*): Well, I can understand your wanting your opinions to be heard as well. I just have a lot of strong feelings about this issue 'cause I have to work hard to get money together to go out.

DELORES: I can understand that. I actually don't mind sharing in the expenses with a date. I'm not sure how the other girls feel about it, though. I just don't like it when guys ask you out and because they're paying and everything, they never ask what you might want to do and then they act like we owe 'em something for treating us. I'd rather pay my way and have it fifty-fifty all the way. And I think your talking so strongly and interrupting me made me feel again that what I have to say doesn't count.

MIKE (*looking at Delores*): I'm sorry. I didn't mean to shut you out. I guess I was reacting to my getting angry at all the silent expectations guys get when it comes to dating. It's actually nice to hear a girl say she wouldn't mind sharing in expenses. And frankly I'd prefer to do something on a date that both of us would like.

TEACHER: Mike, you said it was nice to hear a girl say she wouldn't mind sharing expenses. Do you mean Delores or girls in general?

MIKE (*looking at the teacher*): I mean Delores.

TEACHER (*looking at Mike*): Can you tell her personally?

MIKE (*looking at Delores*): I like your attitude about sharing expenses. It makes me think that you and maybe other girls don't always expect us guys to put out all the money. (*Looking at the class*) I would like to know what other girls in the class have to say about that.

Notice in the above example that the teacher points out a tendency for students to look at her rather than at the person or persons to whom the communication is directed. This enforces and encourages a norm of direct person-to-person communication in the class. The teacher directs students to give eye contact to the person or persons to whom they are speaking. In addition, the teacher directs attention to students in the class by having one student identify by name the individual or several individuals to whom he/she is speaking. Once the teacher has monitored the communication so it is free-flowing and directed toward class members, she is no longer needed and students talk to each other.

Monitoring the communication of a few students in several interactions will establish a norm of direct and free communication. If you establish this norm early, you will not have to continually monitor conversations as the group progresses. Conversely, if you don't establish the norm early, then you may never get students talking directly and freely to each other. You will likely have to do a lot of talking, filtering what every student says through you. If you are inconsistent in monitoring communication and only do it every once in a while, you are likely to constantly be working at trying to establish the norm of direct and free communication.

Shared Responsibility

The first example above involving Charles and Andy serves to identify another norm for building a supportive and helping environment in your peer helping class—namely, that of sharing responsibility for what takes place in the class. If you recall, Charles and Andy were having a side conversation in class, and that became a topic for the whole class to discuss. Each person was invited by the teacher to say how they felt about side conversations. The teacher personalized the issue by asking how individuals in the class feel when someone is whispering or chuckling to someone next to them while they are talking. From such a discussion, an agreement may emerge that side conversations are to be avoided. Some peer helping classes don't rule out such conversations, but rather require those talking aside to share what they said when asked. Regardless of what rule or guideline or agreement is reached, the process of the whole class sharing in establishing it exemplifies the idea of shared responsibility in the group.

Another way in which the group shares responsibility for the class is in taking a role in initiating discussion and deciding on topics and activities for the class. There are a host of topic areas that can be appropriately addressed in a peer helping class. Asking students what they would like to talk about and what they would like to learn will increase their interest and involvement in the class. The best way to do this is to make a list of as many possible topics as you can think of. Distribute the list to students and ask if they have other topics they want to add. You could then have students check off those topics they would like to address in class, or get their verbal input regarding choices. You may want to identify those topic areas that you think are important for the class (e.g., communication skills, problem-solving, self- and other-awareness, interpersonal sensitivity, conflict management, suicide, etc.). You will probably want to include some topics and activities even though students may not prefer them. As long as you solicit student input and ideas in organizing part of the class, you are promoting the norm of shared responsibility.

We encourage you to set up one day each week (if your class meets daily) to hold an open discussion commonly known as an "I feel" session. Here students can talk about whatever they want with an emphasis on personal issues, concerns and problems. Organizing an open talk session gives students an opportunity to support and help each other. It also sets a model for the class being a place where students are invited to talk about personal problems. In doing this, students have opportunity to apply what they have learned in such areas as communication skills, interpersonal sensitivity, cultural awareness, active listening, respecting differences, problem-solving, and conflict management. The open discussion period also gives the class a chance to build many of the growth factors that make your peer helping class helpful.

"Open discussion" is just that. Students take responsibility for the discussion. You stay out of trying to establish a topic and literally remain silent while students consider what they want to share and talk about. If many students want to talk about their personal issues, you may need to organize class time so each one gets a chance. To do this, before the discussion begins, ask who would like to raise a personal concern during the open session. Then try to parcel the time so each person gets group attention. Of course, you need to refrain from cutting students short when a personal issue is raised, so be prepared to continue the open discussion in the next class session.

Once a class becomes familiar with how the open discussion period works, you may find students want to spend increasingly more time just talking with each other. That outcome is to be encouraged and supported. You may need to balance personal discussion time with subject material you want to teach, but ideally once personal discussion gets going, students do a lot in teaching each other. In essence, then, your class becomes a helping environment where students take responsibility for the discussion. In fact, many peer helping teachers will provide more class time for open discussion as the class progresses. You, as leader, facilitate and monitor the discussion. The learning takes place as students give each other help and practice their communication skills as part of the discussion.

Perhaps the most important norm for any peer helping group is that each member's freedom and responsibility to comment on the immediate feelings they experience toward other members and the group as a whole is supported. Providing an open discussion facilitates that process, letting class members know that what they think and feel in interaction and involvement with each other is important to share and talk about.

Self-Disclosure

Peer helping is unique in its focus on the personal lives of students in the class. Curriculum for the class typically focuses students on becoming aware of the self, their values and interests, feelings and preferences, needs and wants. Subject material also focuses on communication and listening skills, interpersonal relations, social skills, conflict management, feeling expression, parent-child relationships, teacher-student relationships and other interpersonal aspects. Topics of concern to youth are usually a major focus, including dating and sexuality, drug use and abuse, suicide, pregnancy, respecting others, appreciating cultural and racial differences, eating disorders, depression, loneliness, career exploration, group belonging and cliques, family conflict, divorce, alcoholism, managing stress, and many others. Given this array of personally meaningful topics, students are likely to talk about themselves and share even intimate feelings and experiences. Such self-disclosure on the part of students should be encouraged.

Self-disclosure is the means whereby students give and receive empathy, acceptance, sympathy, support, advice, encouragement and other forms of help. Without it, your class becomes topic-driven and will lack personal relevance. Through disclosing themselves, learning how to help, and interacting in the class, students come to understand how to talk to and help others with personal problems. They experience it in the class first. From this experience, some students will be able to work effectively as peer helpers for others in the school.

To build the norm of self-disclosure, you need to invite it in your class. Activities that call for self-disclosure are one important way to encourage it. You can also support self-disclosure by acknowledging and reinforcing students when they do disclose. Here are some suggestions for reinforcing self-disclosure:

- Thank a student who shares personal information:

"Jane, I appreciate your opening up to tell us about how sad you feel about your mother's illness. Thank you for sharing that with us."

- Comment on what a student discloses:

"Luann, your struggle to get your friends to stop all their drinking at parties isn't an easy one when no one else feels that way. It takes courage to stand up for what you think is right and try to influence your friends because you care about them and don't want to lose them."

- Ask or direct students to comment on or share reactions to what a student has said about him or herself:

"Kim has really taken a risk to tell us about how she often feels alone and neglected at school. I wonder if any of you have felt similarly at school or in other settings? How does Kim's telling you this affect you? How do you feel about it? Is there anything you want to say to help?"

- Reflect on what it might have been like for a student to share personal information:

"Felice, it looks like it was hard for you to tell us about your father losing his job and the problems that has created for your family. You seem real sad and discouraged about it. And I also sense you could use some support from the class. It's risky putting yourself out there and letting others in on what may be a difficult problem for you and your family.

- Give a "me, too" disclosure in response to a student's personal disclosure:

"Delroy, your talking about how you don't get any support or encouragement from home reminded me of how I never got much help or encouragement from my parents when I wanted to go to college. I felt I was all on my own, and it was hard to believe that I had the ability to make it."

Self-disclosure can sometimes be difficult to handle in a peer helping class. Too much intimate self-disclosure early in the semester can make the class feel too personally demanding. Students who have not disclosed as much as others early in the class may feel pressured to open up before they are ready. Avoid forced disclosure. Students need to work at becoming comfortable with and trusting of each other before they can open up about intimate details in their lives. Nevertheless, don't discourage intimate disclosure early in the class. It sets a norm of openness in the class that will build empathy and trust.

What about The Big Secret? Sometimes students may open up about a personal issue or problem that you and/or the class perceive as being highly intimate or sensitive. A student may state in the class that he/she is homosexual. Telling about being pregnant is another example. Disclosing a problem with drugs or alcohol is an intimate problem. Incest, violent behavior, illegal acts, promiscuous behavior, and a dysfunctional family are other examples. For some, the act of disclosing some deep and hidden secret may be a relief and helpful in and of itself. Those who hear it may not know how to respond, or may be hesitant to share an unwanted response. Typically, when one discloses something deeply personal, others want to ask all sorts of questions about it. How did it happen? When does it happen? How did it start? What makes you keep doing it? While these questions may help the discloser to open up more, they generally serve to satisfy the curiosity of those who ask them. Nevertheless, students can ask whatever they want. **The only important rule to follow is that the person being asked does not have to answer it. Anyone can pass at any time without judgment.**

In addition to encouraging questions and exploration that go deeper into an intimate subject, it is also useful to direct attention to how the disclosure was made and the impact it had on those who heard it. For example, if in a discussion of sexuality and pregnancy Judy tells the class that she is pregnant, you can move the class away from their natural curiosity about it (how it happened, who the guy is, and what she will do about it) to what it is like to tell the class. You might ask the following:

"Judy, you've told us that you're over six weeks pregnant. What made you take the risk to tell the class now? How do you feel telling this to the class? How do you imagine people in the class are feeling about what you said? How would you like them to respond?"

To other listening students you could ask:

"What was it like to hear this from Judy? How can you respond in a helpful and supportive manner to Judy? What kind of feelings does it bring up in you? If you were to disclose something like this about yourself, what might that be like? How would you like the class to respond if you told about something equally sensitive?"

Bringing the focus of discussion to the immediate situation of what is happening in the class because of the disclosure is more helpful to both the discloser and the class. Judy may or may not want advice about what to do, and she may not want to go into more detail. Also, intimate disclosure can raise apprehension in those who receive it, and that needs to be discussed before getting deeper into an already anxiety-arousing subject.

It is very important that students not be ridiculed or in any way punished for disclosing. It can happen that something an individual disclosed previously is brought up later in the heat of an argument or conflict. For example:

"No wonder you're so alone, Frank. All you do is sit back and make faces at what everyone says in the class."

"Rachel, you really make me angry when you're always putting Jackie down. Maybe that's why you get beaten at home."

You should react to such statements immediately and strongly. Point out that a breach of trust has been made. Something that was said in another context with trust in the group was used against the person disclosing it. You can ask the group how they feel about it or how they might feel if this happened to them. You can also point out how this is not a fair way to argue or give feedback or fight. Tell the group that if such things are allowed to happen it will ruin trust in the group and discourage others to open up about personal issues. You can also help the person misusing another's disclosure by directing his/her attention to the impact this likely has on the discloser and others in the class. You can also explore the purpose such misuse of personal disclosure has in the conflict.

Intervening immediately when misuse of personal disclosure occurs is important. Everything else should be held for later discussion. This communicates to the class that personal disclosure will be protected and valued. Safety in disclosing is an important standard for everyone in the class to see.

Valuing the Group

The more important the class is to you and the students, the more helpful and effective it will be. There are many ways in which you can demonstrate your valuing the group and supporting this norm.

Starting the class on time demonstrates value for the time the class meets. Some teachers use the early part of a class for "school or class business." Some of that may be necessary, but often a lot that goes on in those initial minutes can be taken care of after class or in another context. If you arrive late to class or take time during class to talk to individuals (excluding the group), the class will take on a laid-back atmosphere in reflection of your own style. It may take more time getting the class focused on issues or topics of importance. While developing comfort in the class is important and a laid-back style may facilitate that, starting on time communicates the value you place on class time and activity. When you start on time, students will be on time and they will come ready to get involved in class activities and material.

Another way to support a sense of valuing the class is to reinforce comments students may make about the class. Providing opportunities for students to talk about how the class has been helpful and how it can be improved also communicates to them that their experience in the class is important. Sharing your own thoughts and feelings about the class, particularly when you are excited about it or feel good about what is going on, sets a model for others to follow.

Maintaining continuity from one class session to another also shows your support of the class. Establish continuity by organizing topics and material so that they build on each other. Referring to what students have said in prior meetings also helps. If the class has had a rather intense experience one day, talking about that the next day before going on to something new reinforces the connection between sessions and shows your sense of value for the class' experiences. You could say, for example,

> "Yesterday we discussed some difficult issues about people's religious views, and that touched off some strong feelings. While we seemed to be able to work through what came up, I'm wondering how the class is feeling today."

It will benefit the class to re-connect individuals who have been in conflict, helping them see that their conflict has been fully worked through and resolved.

> "Peter, you seem to have little to say to Benjamin since your conflict with him last week. I'd like to know how you are feeling now about Benjamin and what took place then."

Summarizing and evaluating what has taken place during a class session can also support your sense of value for the group. Some peer helping teachers will call on a student to summarize each session at the end. Having students evaluate a session both in terms of what has been good and what may need further attention evidences the importance you place on class activity.

You play an important role in working to establish norms and rules that promote a safe environment for your students to support and help each other. To do this you can facilitate direct and free communication and reinforce students' personal self-disclosure. Invite students to share in taking responsibility for the group and valuing their experience in it. You may wish to establish other norms and rules for your class, but those presented here should be a basis for all others.

Chapter 8

Techniques and Skills
of Group Leadership

Knowledge of group process, group development and norm formation shapes the foundation for group leadership skills. Several skills have been described in previous chapters. Here we review some of those skills in addition to presenting new ones.

Empathic Responding

Otherwise known as active listening, empathic responding teaches students how to make reflective responses. In reflections, the listener picks up the essence of what another is saying and gives that back. In help-intended communication, listeners are encouraged to give reflections that emphasize the speaker's feelings. Reflections essentially communicate: "I'm listening closely to you and this is what I hear you saying."

For example, Kathy says:

> "I'm feeling really upset about my grades. There's so much going on in my life that makes school so hard now. My father's illness has

really upset everybody and my mother has gone back to working full time. I have to help around the house a lot more and my brother is just a real pain with the way he's dealing with everything. I just can't seem to keep up."

Sarah, the listener, reflects:

"You seem really frustrated that all the stress in your family has interfered with your studying and being able to work for high grades like you used to."

Empathic responding can best be learned by first having students pick up feelings that a speaker expresses or finding the feelings expressed in written statements. You could ask everyone in the class to write down something about themselves about which they have feelings that they would be willing to tell the class. It could be a personal concern or problem or some difference between how they are and how they would like to be (for example, "Ideally, I'd like to be more outgoing and have more fun at parties. But in reality, I tend to be shy and sit off somewhere by myself and not have a good time.") Have a couple students read their statements while the class listens for feeling words or thinks about how that individual feels. Then have class members call out the feelings, checking with the person reading the statement as to accuracy. Then have students use the feelings accurately identified to make reflective statements (for example, "You sound annoyed and frustrated with yourself because you want to have a good time at parties, but you get anxious and uncomfortable and want to hide").

Open vs. Closed Questions

- Open questions generally start with "how," "why" or "what."

- Closed questions usually begin with "do," "is," "can," "have," or "will," which result in a "yes," "no," "maybe" or other short-answer response.

Open questions tend to gather more information than closed questions and allow the person more freedom in how to respond. For example, in response to Kathy's statement above, a closed question might be:

"Do you feel angry that your father's illness has caused all this turmoil in your life?"

Whereas an open question might be:

"How do you feel about your father's illness and all the change that has brought about in your family?"

Question Tag

A good way to teach the difference between open and closed questions is play Question Tag (Goodman and Esterly, 1988). Arrange students in small four- to six-person groups. Instruct the group to first ask only closed questions (yes, no, maybe, short answer) of each other. One person asks another person a closed question. The person questioned gives a short-answer response, and then asks a closed question of another person. The group continues this Question Tag with

117

closed questions for about five minutes. Then the group switches to asking only open-ended questions (that is, questions that cannot be answered by a yes, no, maybe or short answer). Question Tag continues for another five minutes or so.

When groups are finished, ask them what they notice are the differences between the two types of questions. How do they feel asking closed questions? How do they feel asking open questions? How do they feel being asked closed vs. open questions? What do they notice is the difference in conversation created by closed and open-ended questions in the group?

Modeling

Students in peer helping classes learn new behaviors by observing you, guest speakers, people presented on film and other media, and especially their peers. Peers are particularly good models because students identify with each other. Only their peers truly understand what it's like to be a teenager—to have demands and expectations placed on them by adults, to have to develop themselves toward some future career, to struggle for social acceptance and intimacy, and to find an acceptable place in school as a student. Adolescents are strong models for each other in the way they dress, act, feel and even think. What one highly respected peer thinks is "cool" is invariably thought of as cool, regardless of what you or any other adult may logically think. Adolescent peers are powerful models for each other; there's no getting around it.

You will observe modeling of both desirable and undesirable behavior. The class clown gets attention by acting silly or saying comical things in class. That may be a way of breaking the ice, bringing humor to boredom, or merely getting attention. Some of the acting out is likely to appeal to most adolescents. If you try to suppress it altogether, you're likely to be seen as stuffy and intolerant of their "just being human," and possibly lose some respect from students. On the other hand, if you allow too much humor, or if this becomes a primary way for students to get recognition in your class, you may find yourself constantly interrupted by several individuals clowning for attention. That's why it is important for you to give selective attention and reinforcement to students who exhibit behaviors you deem desirable. Your attention and acknowledgment of those who act in the most acceptable manner is a way of setting up appropriate peer models in your class. If you laugh at some students' humorous comments, you will communicate that humor is fun and acceptable in class. If you confront a student who is joking too much or is always humorous (e.g., "Edward, your cracking jokes is sometimes funny, but since you constantly do it, I'd like for you to find other ways of expressing yourself in class"), you establish that humor is acceptable, but not all the time and not as the only manner of expression.

You will be a good model depending on the respect students hold for you. If you tend to be open, accepting, warm, non-judgmental, tolerant, empathic, and interesting, students are likely to model these qualities after you, based on the respect you've earned from them. Students like people who treat them in this manner. On the other hand, if you demand respect through a more authoritative stance (e.g., strict adherence to rules, stern consequences to rule-breaking, harsh voice tones, doling out punishment, openly criticizing, name-calling), you will likely get compliance, but not respect. Consequently, students are less likely to model other behaviors you exhibit and want them to imitate.

A lot of learning takes place through observing others. Hearing a student talk about common difficulties and hearing particularly helpful suggestions about how to handle the problem or deal with feelings provide models for other students. Students can try out new ways of coping with problems as presented by other students. If it works, the student wins. If not, at least the student attempted a new behavior.

Silence

Remaining silent is rarely thought of as a conversational skill, but it is in fact a subtly powerful one. Silence is the giving of space while maintaining attention with the eyes, ears, and body. In giving another or an entire class silent space, you as the class leader give them opportunity to think things over and time to experience the depth of their feelings.

Silent space is also helpful in furthering the norms of free interaction and shared responsibility. If you always have something to say when there is a pause in the classroom, students will learn to become dependent on your filling up all spaces. They'll also become more passive and look to you to direct and entertain them. If you allow silence, even long extended silent spaces, you let students know that it is important for them to respond, that you want to hear from them, and that you will give them plenty of time in which to gather their thoughts before speaking.

Teachers who have strong needs for control or who have overbearing personalities or who can't tolerate the discomfort of silent spaces will have difficulty exercising this skill. But if you identify yourself in this manner, you are more than likely one who needs to practice silence. We're often surprised to find how many peer helping teachers have not learned the basic teaching skill of asking an open-ended question and then sitting in silence waiting for a response. Inevitably, if you wait long enough, someone in the class will comment, even in a group of predominantly quiet, shy people.

So think of silence as a gift you give others—as attentive nonverbal support. When you give silence, your students will move to deeper levels of emotional experience. They will also become more thoughtful about what they say. Unfortunately, the opposite occurs when there is little silent space in a group. Group members rarely express feelings or do so in a circumspect manner. Conversation tends to be more superficial. Students give less quality attention to each other and tend to shift from one topic to another. Silence is, in fact, so powerful and effective that sometimes it is good to direct your students to be silent and "feel into" what was just said, or to think deeply about how to express themselves before speaking.

You can teach the importance of silence to your class through the following exercise:

1. Organize your class into small groups of six to eight members. Separate the groups sufficiently so they won't interfere with each other.

2. Have the groups decide on one or two topics they would like to discuss. You could make

the topics relevant to a topic area you have been working on in the class, or reactions to a film or speaker, or feelings about something that recently happened in the class or on campus.

3. The groups then discuss the topic in two five- to seven-minute segments. In the first segment, the rule is to allow absolutely no silence between talking turns. Each student must take responsibility to say something immediately after another has finished talking. Students can stay on the topic chosen or go wherever their discussion leads.

4. For the second discussion segment, students continue talking about the chosen topic, but now they must leave a silent space of at least ten seconds between talking turns. That is, after one student stops talking, everyone in the group must wait ten seconds before another student starts to talk, even if the student gives only a brief, one-word response. It is best to assign one student in each group to time the silent spaces. Rarely are students able to stick to the ten-second rule, but they can do as best they can.

5. With members remaining in their small groups, lead a whole-class discussion on the topic of silence vs. non-silence. Put the words "silence" and "non-silence" on the board and ask students to comment about what they noticed and experienced in each discussion.

Write a summary of student comments under each heading. Here's our sample of what students usually discover:

Silence	No Silence
More Feelings	Rapid Discussion
More Personal	Excited Discussion
Warmer Tone	Discomfort
Stay on One Topic	Too Many Topics
More Concern	Laughter
More Thought	Superficial Conversation
Less Frustrating	Less Meaningful
	Less Personal
	Frustrating
	Impatience

Chaining

Connecting one individual to another or several individuals to each other is called chaining. You link students to each other by drawing attention to some commonalty they share, similarly held views, parallel experiences, and even potential conflicts. Here are some examples of linking expressions:

> "Sally, you seem to have feelings similar to Jamie's about this issue."

> "Steve, I gather from your comments that you agree with Mike and Andrea about what the class should be doing right now."

> "Cynthia, your feelings about school sound like they are directly opposite those expressed by Ed and Althea. Could you say more about how you see things differently?"

Chaining is a technique that you can use throughout the time you are leading your peer helping group. It is particularly helpful in building cohesiveness in early stages of the class. When students see that their views or ideas or feelings are similar to others' in the group and they get a chance to express this, it builds a sense of belonging through shared experiences. Chaining, when used skillfully, enables you to get individuals in your class to talk to each other. You comment about their similarities or differences and let them go into talking further. An important skill in group leadership involves facilitating group member interaction; chaining is a major tool for accomplishing this.

Process Observation and Comment

Focusing on how the group is operating, the way individuals are talking or functioning, will highlight here-and-now processes that occur in the group. The group process includes patterns, repeated events and sequences of behavior. Commenting on processes you observe draws group member attention to what is happening in the here-and-now for their observation, reflection and comment. As group members become aware of their own patterns and processes, they can make informed choices in changing or continuing them. Here are some examples of process comments from a group leader:

> "I notice that whenever anyone asks a question, several members of the class look at me. I gather that many of you are looking to me for answers and perhaps missing valuable contributions you can give to each other."

> "It seems like the silence we're experiencing today in our share time stands in sharp contrast to the deep personal discussion we had yesterday. I wonder what people are feeling in the silence and how that might relate to yesterday's session."

> "We seem to have adopted a rule that only positive feelings can be disclosed and negative ones avoided."

> "I'd like to point out a pattern that I've observed in the group. Whenever I ask a question, the same three people eagerly respond with their ideas or feelings. While I appreciate their enthusiasm, I also sense that even though we talked about wanting to hear from more

people and wanting to help others talk more, we have difficulty putting this into action."

"Jane, you looked away to Ellen when Jim told you what you did that made him angry. I wonder what you're feeling right now."

Effective process comments will draw the focus of discussion to the immediate feelings, thoughts and experiences of group members. As mentioned in earlier chapters, here-and-now focus brings the group closer together and brings group members into an immediate experience of each other. This facilitates openness, trust and cohesiveness in the group.

Your efforts to master these and other group leadership skills will offer beneficial outcome to all members of your class. We encourage your deliberate efforts to implement these important skills.

Chapter 9

What Do I Do When...?

Each peer helping class is a little different from the previous one, and each class brings new challenges. When conducting workshops, I (JS) am frequently asked, "What do I do when...?" While the questions vary to a certain degree, I find some of the same ones are asked over and over, just in different locations.

In anticipation of your needing some of these same answers, we will discuss ten of the most commonly asked questions in this chapter.

What Do I Do When...

...the Class Wants a Student Removed?

Ms. Ward, a peer helping teacher, called me (JS) one night on the phone to discuss this exact question. She stated that one of the students was a troublemaker in class: rowdy, obnoxious, and just generally unpleasant to be around. When this girl (we will call her Alice) had the flu and was absent for several days, a group of students got together and decided the class was much better without her. They approached their teacher and asked her to talk to Alice about leaving the class. Ms.

Ward admitted that the students were right about the class being a more cohesive group when Alice was away. This peer helping group met after school and did not receive credit for the training, so Ms. Ward felt she could ask Alice to leave without jeopardizing her academic progress. However, Ms. Ward had enough doubts about asking Alice to leave to cause her to place a phone call to me.

I asked Ms. Ward several questions after she told me the story. My first question was, "What is your purpose in having a peer helping class?"

Her response was, "To train students to help each other."

I then asked, "What type of students do you want them to help?"

"All types, of course."

"All types, except Alice?"

"I guess I hadn't looked at it in that light," she responded.

We then talked about how Alice would feel if she was asked to leave the peer helping class. Was she having trouble in her other classes? Had she entered peer helping thinking she would find acceptance in a group of nonjudgmental peers? If she didn't find acceptance here, where would she find it? If there were not people in peer helping who cared enough to help Alice, where would she find caring people?

Also, if a class felt they had the power to exclude students, how would this affect their self-perception? Would they soon begin to think of themselves as an elite group? Would peers who needed help seek out peers who were viewed as a clique on campus?

In thinking about these questions and hearing her own answers, Ms. Ward decided it would be incorrect to ask Alice to leave the class. She decided to talk to the students who had made the request and ask them some of the same questions I had asked her. She felt confident they would come to the same conclusion she had. Also, she was going to ask students to brainstorm ways they could work together in reaching out to Alice in a positive way.

Ms. Ward is not the only teacher who has asked our opinion on how to handle a disruptive or difficult student. We feel there may be others experiencing the same or a similar situation and would like to have the subject discussed. We advocate the following principles and steps in addressing the disruptive or unwanted student in a peer helping class:

1. Encourage and help students in the class to give specific feedback that will help the problem student to change and become more acceptable. Feedback should focus on specific behaviors that are problematic and the impact those behaviors have on students in the group. Feedback should also include concrete suggestions for how students would like that individual to act.

2. Reinforce the identified student for positive changes he or she makes, while encouraging change in areas needing improvement. Help students to also acknowledge positive changes. Generally, these two steps should eliminate anyone from being excluded from your class.

3. It could occur that after much feedback, reinforcement, and encouragement, someone still disrupts the progress of the group. In that case, tell the person how he/she has to change to stay in the class. Give him/her time to improve before you move to exclusion.

4. Always make every effort to keep a student in the class and help students to work with the disruptive individual in a constructive manner. Often students want a troublesome member removed from class so they can avoid conflict and uncomfortable confrontation. But this type of conflict and confrontation is exactly what helps students—both the problem person and other group members—grow and learn. So, always make every effort to keep students in the class in whatever way you can. Everyone in the class will likely gain from your efforts.

5. If all effort fails, you need to recognize that some students may be damaged by being allowed or forced to stay in the class. There may be a rare student who cannot benefit from peer feedback and cannot make appropriate changes. Indeed, an occasional student may become more dysfunctional in the class with peer feedback that is given in a supportive and caring manner. Keeping such a student in the class can be destructive to both the student and the class. You need to be willing to tell a student that he/she is not ready at the present time to benefit from the class experience. Also,

express your concern that the class appears to be damaging to both the student and the class. You may want to include a referral to counseling and/or an invitation to return to another peer helping class if the student feels ready in the future.

...the Group Does Not Advance Quickly Enough?

Our question to this is, "Quickly enough, according to whose standard?" In peer helping the need to be flexible is of the utmost importance. Students do not develop skills according to a rigid timetable. Some units of study which a teacher thinks will take two weeks may, in fact, take double that time. Other units may progress very quickly. It is our belief that peer helpers should always remain in an advanced class as long as they are functioning in a peer helping capacity on campus. Therefore, training is continuous, and some of the pressure is taken off the teacher who feels that every individual in class must be at a certain level of expertise by a designated time.

We must remember that all babies do not walk at the same time. Some may start walking as early as nine months, while others may not walk until the fourteenth or fifteenth month of age. However, by the time they are three years old, children are usually all walking equally well. The same is true of peer helpers. Some just need a little more time than others.

On the other hand, classes should not get bogged down on certain units and stay on those units for months. One teacher complained that she had been unable to proceed on schedule with lessons because students usually got off the subject, and a lot of time was spent on things which were not pertinent. When a situation like this occurs on a regular basis, it is the teacher's responsibility to guide the discussion back to the topic.

Some teachers may expect an unrealistic level of competence from students. Because of their desire for perfection, these teachers may be staying on units much too long. Remember, we are not training "mini-psychiatrists."

...Confidentiality Is Broken?

This will happen at some time or the other, and it may be when least expected. Sometimes confidentiality is broken quite unintentionally. Here is an example:

> Jeanie shared in class that her mother and father were getting a divorce, and she would be moving with her mother to another state. Her brother, Bob, would remain in the city with his father. Larry was in class when Jeanie shared, and he presumed Bob also knew about the pending arrangement. When Larry saw Bob on campus, he told Bob that he thought it was great he was getting to remain with his father and continue in their school.

> Much to Larry's amazement, Bob had not been told that his mother and sister were leaving. At this point Larry realized that he had broken confidentiality. He reported his breach of trust to the class the following day, and Jeanie was very upset that he had spoken to her brother about things shared in class.

When confidentiality is broken, trust is destroyed. For several weeks, students will be hesitant to open up during sharing time. The class must build up trust again.

When peer helping contracts are signed at the beginning of the semester, the teacher should emphasize the damage that can be done by someone breaking confidentiality. We also suggest that if someone breaks confidentiality, that person should be talked to seriously so he/she will not do it again. However, if someone breaks confidentiality more than one time, you may suggest to that student that peer helping may not be the right place to remain. A peer helping class cannot function effectively if trust is constantly being destroyed by someone who cannot keep confidentiality. In order to maintain the trust class members have in each other, you must be willing to remove a student from the class when he/she *repeatedly* breaks confidentiality.

...One Person Wants to Dominate?

You will want to make certain that you do not encourage a dominating student by calling on him/her more frequently than you do other students. Often the dominating student will be the first to volunteer and may be more aggressive in keeping the spotlight on him/herself. A skilled teacher will not ignore a dominating student, but will seek out the quiet students and make certain they have equal opportunity to join conversations.

If one student is dominating on a routine basis, you may ask two students in class to tactfully speak to the dominating student and express their concern about some students not having an opportunity to be heard.

Periodically, ask students in a general class discussion how they feel the class is progressing. Students may say, without mentioning names or pointing a finger in a negative way, that they would like to see a limit put on the time a student can speak.

We believe that students are more effective than teachers in changing the behavior of their peers. By receiving positive peer pressure, a student will probably make a more conscientious effort to change than if he/she thinks a "teacher is on his case." Students are effective in helping each other. This is something the peer helping teacher should always remember, especially when confronted with a student who has a tendency to dominate in class.

...There Is a Need for a Substitute Teacher?

Because of their bond with the teacher and the confidentiality aspect of peer helping, students often feel uncomfortable when they arrive in class and find the regular teacher absent and a substitute filling in. However, it is unrealistic to think that a peer helping teacher will never be ill and never have to miss days of school.

In anticipation of someday being absent, there are steps a teacher can take to ease the anxiety of students.

> 1. Discuss with the students what activities they would feel comfortable doing with a substitute teacher. For example, they would probably choose to postpone their "I feel..." (sharing day) until the regular teacher returned. They might choose to work in small groups or do short plays followed by a discussion.

134

2. You will want to stress the importance of treating the substitute with utmost respect. Remind students of the things they have learned in their unit on meeting a stranger. Stress the value of having a substitute leave with a good impression of the class. Students need to be told of the importance of public relations when peer helping is involved.

3. If you need to be absent for an extended period of time, try to choose your substitute before you leave and brief her/him on what to expect when teaching the class. Most substitutes will look at peer helping as just another class, and, if not given proper instruction, they may become frustrated to discover the class has a different format than their other assignments.

4. Remember to send notes to be read to your class if you are out for an indefinite period. Students will want to know how you are and will appreciate hearing from you.

5. Try to arrange to have the same substitute each time you are away from your class. Some peer helping teachers are able to leave their classes and feel confident that all is well when they are at home ill or away at conferences, jury duty, union-negotiating meetings, or other staff assignments because they have left a familiar, experienced person with their students.

6. Always leave a lesson plan for a substitute in your desk in case you unexpectedly find yourself unable to be at school. The lesson plan can be of a generic nature which would fit with any unit you are currently covering.

7. When you return to class, discuss with your students the previous day's (or days') activities. Ask for their feelings about how things went. If areas of improvement are needed, talk about what changes should be made before a substitute is called again.

8. Emphasize to students that peer helping belongs to them, and they are responsible for making it a good class whether or not you are there.

I (JS) was called to a school where the peer helping teacher was out with a broken hip, and the students were giving the substitute all kinds of trouble. They missed their very popular teacher and were totally unaccepting of the person taking her place. In their eyes she could do nothing right. The substitute was a nice person who had truly tried when she first arrived, but her own frustrations were now beginning to show.

I spent time with the class and the substitute teacher, and I was pleased with the final outcome. The students decided to claim ownership of their class and strive to make it the best they could. They also agreed to extend their practice of being nonjudgmental and accepting to include the substitute.

I saw some of these students at a state conference a couple of months later, and they were very eager to tell me how well the class was going even though the regular teacher had not yet returned. They had assumed responsibility for their own actions and were now taking pride in how successful the class had become.

...a Class Member
(or Another Person on Campus) Dies?

When a death occurs (or any other tragic or emergency situation), the unit of study which is presently being discussed needs to be set aside, and the teacher should immediately turn to the unit on death and dying. If this unit has just recently been covered, then a quick review may be adequate.

Students need time to discuss their feelings, and this process should not be rushed. If the student who died was a peer helping classmate or a student on campus who was known by many of the members in the class, certainly more time should be set aside for sharing, remembering, and grieving.

In the advanced class, students may need a review of how they will be functioning as peer helpers during the forthcoming days. Peer helpers can lead grief/loss group meetings at lunch, which are open to any student who wants to attend. These meetings often draw more students than those led by professionals invited to campus.

Peer helpers in your class may want to contact siblings of the deceased and be available to talk to them. Sometimes younger brothers and sisters are "spared" any details of final arrangements and may feel left out and alone. A peer helper with a good listening ear can be a big help to these young people who are also experiencing grief.

*...a Teacher, Parent or Community Group
Complains about Something Relating to Peer Helping,
and It Is Brought Up in Class?*

Any controversial issue discussed in class should be done so with honesty, tact, and a sense of being nonjudgmental toward the person who is complaining.

You will probably want to explain to the class that most things which have an impact on people (and peer helping certainly falls in this category) will receive both positive and negative comments. Some of the criticism may not be valid, but if it is, the class may want to discuss how they can correct the problem. For example, if a teacher is complaining that students are being taken out of his/her class to see a peer helper, something can be done immediately to eliminate that situation.

Sometimes complaints are made because of a lack of information or even incorrect data. Peer helpers may want to invite to their class a person who allegedly is spreading negative criticism. Sometimes the most harsh complainer makes a complete turnaround after being given VIP treatment and correct information by a group of caring peer helpers. Negative people have been known to become positive supporters.

Learning to deal with negative people can be a valuable lesson for peer helpers. This skill will be useful for the rest of their lives.

...a Member of the Class Rarely Contributes?

We do not believe students should be forced to share before they feel comfortable. Some students come from families who do not talk about feelings. In fact, some students are raised to think that talking about problems is a sign of weakness. Feelings developed in this environment do not go away overnight just because a person has entered a peer helping class. These students may need many months, or sometimes longer, before they can comfortably say anything other than, "I'm fine" or "I pass." If the teacher is patient and viewed as being accepting and nonjudgmental of the nonparticipating student, normally there will come a time when the person will begin to contribute.

If a student is just quiet, and the class is full of extroverts who are eager to talk, then the teacher should make certain the reserved person is given opportunities to join in the discussion. Other students may want to practice their group leadership skills by being sensitive and aware of quiet people in the class and encouraging their comments by using such statements as, "I am in favor of the issue, but I'd be interested to know what Raji thinks because he has lived in that country."

Also, remember that students who rarely contribute may be getting a lot more out of the class than anyone else realizes.

...a New Person Enters the Group Late?

Before a new person arrives, the class should be instructed on what to do when someone joins late. Then, when a student enters the class unexpectedly, there will not be an awkward moment.

You will want to talk about the importance of welcoming a new student to class when you are presenting the lesson "Meeting a Stranger." Since this is usually the first lesson of the semester, students will receive their instruction early and be prepared to reach out to a new person.

Remind students to talk about things the new person is interested in. For example, if a new student has a baseball shirt on, a peer helper can ask the person how he/she feels the team is doing. The peer helper will also want to introduce the stranger to some of his/her friends outside of the peer helping class.

The first day is often the hardest for a student entering school late, and one of the peer helpers can sit with the new person during brunch and lunch. This may be repeated by different peer helpers volunteering on following days.

One peer helper can help the new person get caught up with lessons the class has already covered. This may involve enlisting the help of fellow peer helpers to participate in role-playing situations.

The main thing to remind students is that the peer helping class is not a closed, cliquish club, but rather a warm, inviting place where new students feel welcome and at home.

...a Fight or Other Disturbance Breaks Out in Class?

Normally teachers ask this question before they have been in a peer helping class. Their experience may have been in a classroom where disruptions do occur. However, this type of behavior is very atypical for a peer helping class. Even students who have been known as troublemakers in other classes normally find peer helping to be an accepting place where overt, negative behavior is unnecessary. The positive peer pressure in the room, plus the modeling of acceptance and caring by the teacher, usually sets the tone for proper behavior.

If, however, some unexpected trouble occurs, rules of the school for handling such behavior need to be observed.

Chapter 10

Transferring from One Peer Helping Group to Another

Peer helping groups bond so well that students often speak of their class as being like a family. Therefore, changing from one class to another is a traumatic experience for most students. These changes may occur when a student moves to another school district, to a different school within the same district, to an advanced class, or to a higher level of education, such as going from high school to college. Whenever and wherever the change occurs, students are often unhappy for a period of time.

The teacher will be aware of students' feelings mainly when the beginning group graduates and peers find themselves in different advanced groups, which may be made up of students who were not in the same beginning class. The teacher will likely notice that students are not as open with one another at the beginning as they had been in their original classes. Again trust must be built.

Often students will approach the teacher with comments such as: "I want to get back with my group. This group isn't as good as my old one." Or the comments may be more forthright: "I can't stand being in this new group. It doesn't feel right." Other students may come right out and beg: "Please, put me back with my group. I don't want to stay here."

Students need to be gently reminded that getting acquainted with new students, learning from them, and allowing them to learn from you is what peer helping is all about. Tell them that you understand what they are feeling, and let them know that it is quite normal to feel this way. Reassure them that within a short time the new group probably will feel as comfortable as their old group. In fact, students typically report that after a period of time, they actually like their new group better.

It is important to spend time letting the students get to know each other at the formative stage of any new group, no matter how advanced in skills that group may be. Getting-acquainted games, similar to those used in the beginning class, may again be played. Dividing the students into twos and allowing them to get to know each other is a very important activity. Ask these students to introduce each other to the other members of the class. The same bonding which took place in the beginning class will soon start to happen in the advanced class.

You will probably want to have a retreat or an evening function where all the peer helpers from the school come together. The friendships which have been made in previous groups will be renewed as friends see each other again.

It may be somewhat easier for a peer helper to move to a new school in another district than it is to change groups in the same school. When a person moves to a new school, he/she makes an extra effort to reach out and make new friends. The student realizes that returning to the original peer helping class is impossible, so he/she does not dwell on that thought.

When a student moves to a new school, he/she is often so happy to find a peer helping class available that the pain of leaving the old group is somewhat diminished. Fortunately, peer helping has spread to so many schools that it is easier to find classes than it was a few years ago.

Probably one of the most difficult times to leave a peer helping group is when a student graduates from high school. The group may have been together for several years, and the students realize that each person will be going his/her own separate way. Some will go on to college, and a few may become a part of a peer helping program on a college campus. Being a part of that group may be an entirely different experience than belonging to the previous high school group, but the peer helper is usually able to meet the new challenges. Inviting two or three of these college students back as speakers to your class is a good experience for them and for your peer helpers.

Changing from one group to another is never easy, but peer helpers, because of their training, are probably more adept at it than most students. They may complain and express a desire to stay with their original group, but within weeks, peer helpers usually have made the adjustment and are ready to continue their work.

Encourage students to seek peer helping groups in the work settings, schools, colleges, or universities they will attend. If there is no peer helping program at that new site, encourage them to start one. Your efforts to help might be the basis for peer helping to begin in an entirely new setting.

Chapter 11

Models of Peer Helping Groups

Peer helping groups come in many different shapes and forms. One of the reasons peer helping has spread so rapidly is probably because of its ability to be adapted to fit various schedules on different campuses. This chapter will look at some of the different models of peer helping groups.

An Elective Class That Meets on a Daily Basis

This group will meet for one period every school day. The class will be listed on the master schedule like other electives, and students will sign up for the class. The number of students admitted to the class may vary from one school district to another. Some classes may be limited to twenty or twenty-five students, and others may allow thirty to thirty-five students to enroll.

Since this is a regular class meeting during the school day, a grade and credit will be given. The class will appear on each student's transcript. This record may prove to be valuable when a student is looking for a job as a resident assistant in a college dormitory or a camp counselor. Because of their listening skills, peer helpers are often chosen for these jobs over other students.

Peer helpers in this group usually will be expected to write journals, read books and give reports, take tests, participate in class activities and projects. This class is definitely not just a "rap session."

It is best to have both beginning and advanced classes. Varying with districts, students may be allowed to stay in the advanced group for two, four, or more semesters.

An Elective Class That Meets Before or After School

Many schools refer to this time as "zero period." While it is not in the school day proper, it is still looked upon as a regular class which carries all the privileges of the ones meeting during the day.

Students receive a grade and credit for this class, and the grade is placed on the transcript. The same requirements will be expected of this class as are expected in the previously mentioned peer helping class.

Because some students have an extremely busy schedule, they may choose to take peer helping at zero period because it is the only time during the day they can work it into their schedule. The before-school time often proves more popular than the afternoon schedule because of conflicts with after-school activities.

A Noncredit Course That Meets at Noon, Before, or After School

This group may meet only once or twice a week. While students basically cover the same material as those in the credit classes (it just takes longer), they do not receive credit.

Some teachers really enjoy leading a group of this type. Their comments are: "I don't have to worry about giving grades, and it gives me more time to work with my students." Or, "The schoolday is over and the students are remaining at school because they choose to be there."

Because of the limited time placed on these groups, it has always been our opinion that teachers should work toward getting their noncredit classes into the normal school day. Meeting every day not only gives the class more consistency, but there is real value in the teacher meeting with the students on a daily basis. However, if the administration will allow peer helping to function on campus only at noon, before, or after school, then it is certainly better to have it at those times than not to have it at all.

Teachers leading this type of group must be careful to avoid burnout. Because they are already teaching their regularly scheduled periods, they add this extra assignment on top of everything else. Even if they are only meeting a day or two a week, the peer helpers are probably seeking them out daily for guidance. This is especially true of the advanced group, who see peers and will need supervision.

A Week of Concentrated Training or a Weekend Retreat

Some teachers meet with students for an entire week before school starts in the fall. During this time students supposedly become trained to function as peer helpers on campus. Other teachers meet with students on a weekend retreat, and a limited amount of training is given.

Compacted training of this type should be just a kick-off to further ongoing training when students return to campus. However, if it is meant to be the total training, and the teacher only supervises students on campus, there may be real danger ahead. The importance of ongoing training cannot be over-emphasized.

Pullout Classes Using Alternating Periods

Some schools cannot have a period set aside for peer helping, and the teacher may find it necessary to pull students out of a regular class. Since students cannot be taken from the same period each time, the pullout periods are alternated. A teacher may have peer helping first period one week, second period the next week, third period the following week, and so on. Of course, the person teaching must be a counselor or teacher not assigned to regular teaching periods. These classes are usually small, with only eight to ten members.

No matter which type of group you have, each will bring its own challenges. Your need for group leadership skills is apparent in teaching any of these groups. While the settings and times of meetings are different on various campuses, the hope is that the outcome will be the same: peer helpers will be adequately trained and supervised to allow them to help their peers.

Chapter 12

Helpful Reminders

I (JS) was recently talking to a friend who commented, "There are a couple of kids in my peer helping class that I'm concerned about. They are quiet and rarely contribute to the group. I just wonder if they are getting anything out of the class."

I had to smile as I remembered I once had the same concerns about a few students in my peer helping classes. But an incident happened sometime later that made me realize I should not try to judge who is and is not getting something out of the class. I told her the following story.

> Raymond was a good kid, but one who seemed to be apathetic to life. He came to class every day, did what the course required, but never seemed to get the spark for peer helping that most students have. He completed his beginning training and requested the advanced class. I kept hoping to see a fire kindled under him, but that never happened. He graduated in the spring and I lost track of him. But every once in a while I would remember him and wonder if he had gotten anything out of peer helping.

Several years passed before I saw Raymond again. One Friday night at the school's homecoming football game, he approached me with a smile and an extended hand.

"Mrs. Sturkie," he said, "I'm so glad to see you."

"I'm glad to see you, too, Raymond," I responded. "I've wondered about you."

"I'm in my third year of college, majoring in physical education. Wanta be a coach someday."

"That's great. Maybe you will coach on this football field."

"I don't know about that, but I will definitely coach someplace. I've got to run now, but before I leave I just want to tell you how important peer helping was to me my last year in school."

Seeing the quizzical look on my face, he continued, "I know you probably think I didn't get much out of the class because I didn't join in the conversations most of the time. Don't guess I even showed much interest for what was going on. But that doesn't mean I wasn't listening and learning."

"I'm glad to hear that, Raymond," I stammered. "To be honest, sometimes I did wonder."

"Well, let me quickly tell you what it did for me. You remember I lived alone with my dad."

I nodded.

"We never got along. Most of the time we just tried to avoid each other. That is, until I took peer helping. I tried some of those things we learned in class on my dad, and you know what? They worked."

"You mean things like active listening and sending effective messages?"

"Yea, those things that you said would help us communicate better with our parents. Well, you were right! Dad and I started talking to each other, and we have a pretty close relationship now. Peer helping made the difference. I just wanted you to know that."

With those words, Raymond disappeared into the crowd, and I haven't seen him since. But I have always remembered our brief conversation, and I've been thankful that he took a few minutes to set my thinking straight. Now I believe that others I was in doubt about may have gotten something too. At least, I've stopped trying to judge.

Another friend commented to me that she felt she was not able to do enough after-school activities with her peer helping group. Her family needed her time too. She told me about a young, unmarried teacher who was able to spend a lot of time with her group. On weekends they would do fundraisers such as car washes, bake sales, and even talent shows. On long holiday weekends the group would go to the mountains for retreats. My friend commented that she wished she had the available time to do all of these things with her peer helping class.

I reminded my friend that most peer helping teachers do not have the available time that particular young, single teacher had, and those who do not, need not feel guilty. I also told her I would question whether it is positive or negative for a teacher to become so involved with peer helping students. Could the teacher be lonely and trying to fill a void or a need she has? Would the peer helpers come to depend on the teacher too much because she is always available to them? It is understandable that teachers and peer helpers become good friends, but teachers must also remember they are not there to become buddies to students. There is a fine line which the teacher should not cross.

If you are a busy person with home, family, community, or social commitments as well as school responsibilities, remember that you are probably a better peer helping teacher because of it. Your students probably see you as a good role model, one who balances both professional and private life.

One teacher at a conference expressed concern that her peer helping class seemed to have a lot of conflicts. She had heard that students often refer to their class as a family, and she was afraid her group did not feel as close as what she thought peer helping groups were supposed to.

Groups who never have conflict are probably immature and not growing. In order to have conflict, there is already established a degree of trust, openness, and cohesiveness. Conflict actually produces more maturity in the group because members learn to work through situations.

An analogy to a marriage may apply. When a husband and wife never quarrel, it only means that conflict is not being brought out into the open. Feelings are being "stuffed" and roles are being played to make it look like everything is all right, when actually it is not. If there is enough maturity in the marriage, feelings may be expressed and conflicts worked out. The result is a stronger relationship. The same is true with a peer helping class. However, certain rules must be observed in dealing with the conflict, such as no intentional putdowns, so the conflict does not become a war.

Peer helping teachers train students to recognize that they will not always be successful in their peer helper roles. The same thing applies to the teacher in his/her role. No matter how much you try or how hard you work, there will be times when you will not be as successful in your role as a group leader as you would like to be. As you tell your students, when those times come, you do not feel guilty. You look at the situation and see if there is anything you could have done differently to improve it. If you discover something else you could have done, then the next time, you try it. It may work, and it may not. If you look at the situation and know there was nothing else you could have done differently, you put the experience behind you and move on. Peer helping teachers need to remember that feeling guilty takes energy, and you don't have any of that to spare.

In closing, the final thought that we would like to leave with you is: Lighten up, have fun, and enjoy your peer helping group. Because when you do, the students will also enjoy their experience.

Bibliography

Burton, Robert L. "Group Process Demystified." In *The 1982 Annual for Facilitators, Trainers, and Consultants*. San Diego, California: University Associates, 1982.

Carlock, C. Jesse, and Beverly Byrum-Gaw. "Group Energy, Group Stage, and Leader Interventions." In *The 1982 Annual Handbook for Group Facilitators."* San Diego, California: University Associates, 1982.

Corey, Marianne Schneider, and Gerald Corey. *Groups: Process and Practice.* 4th ed. Monterey, California: Brooks/Cole, 1992.

D'Andrea, Vincent, and Peter Salovey. *Peer Counseling Skills and Perspectives.* Palo Alto, California: Science and Behavior Books, 1983.

Dinkmeyer, D. C., and J. J. Muro. *Group Counseling: Theory and Practice.* 2nd ed. Itasca, Illinois: F. E. Peacock, 1979.

Gazda, G. M. *Group Counseling: A Developmental Approach.* 4th ed. Boston: Allyn & Bacon, 1989.

Goodman, Gerald, and Glenn Esterly. *The Talk Book.* Emmaus: Pennsylvania: Rodale Press, 1988.

Myrick, Robert D., and Don L. Sorenson. *Peer Helping: A Practical Guide.* Minneapolis, Minnesota: Educational Media Corporation, 1988.

Ohlsen, M. M., A. M. Horne, and C. F. Lawe. *Group Counseling.* 3rd ed. New York: Holt, Rinehart & Winston, 1988.

Pearson, Richard E. "Basic Skills for Leadership of Counseling Groups." In *Counselor Education and Supervision* 3, (1981): 30-37.

Rogers, Carl. *Carl Rogers on Encounter Groups.* New York: Harper & Row, 1970.

Schutz, W. C. "The Interpersonal Underworld." In *FIRO: A Three Dimensional Theory of Interpersonal Behavior.* Reprint ed. Palo Alto, California: Science & Behavior Books, 1966.

Sturkie, Joan. *Listening With Love: True Stories From Peer Counseling.* Revised ed. San Jose, California: Resource Publications, Inc., 1989.

Sturkie, Joan, and Marsh Cassady. *Acting It Out.* San Jose, California: Resource Publications, Inc., 1990.

Sturkie, Joan, and Valerie Gibson. *The Peer Helper's Pocketbook.* San Jose, California: Resource Publications, Inc., 1992.

Waldo, Michael. "A Currative Factor Framework for Conceptualizing Group Counseling." *Journal of Counseling and Development* 64, (1985): 52-58.

Yalom, Irvin D. *The Theory and Practice of Group Psychotherapy.* 3rd ed. New York: Basic Books, Inc., 1985.

You Can Help Today's Teenagers!

The Peer Counseling Training Course

by Maggie Phillips,
revised by Joan Sturkie

126 looseleaf pages, $49.95
8½" x 11"
ISBN 0-89390-185-7

The Peer Counseling Training Course is a teacher's guide and complete curriculum for a junior high or high school course in peer helping.

Teenagers often find it easier to talk about their problems and issues with other students than with adults. Through helping other teens identify and talk about their issues, peer helpers also learn something about themselves.

The Peer Counseling Training Course helps you train teens to be there for each other. It is divided into nineteen units. Units one through nine introduce the students to the skills they must learn to be good listeners and "peer helpers." Units ten through nineteen deal with specific problems the students might face, such as peer pressure, drugs, alcohol, etc.

This training course is based on the widely known H.O.L.D. program, which was originally developed by **Maggie Phillips** for the Pajaro Valley Unified School District in Watsonville, California. **Joan Sturkie**, an active consultant for school peer counseling programs, has revised and updated the program.

Order from your local bookseller, or use order form on last page.

Teach Teens to Listen With Love

*Listening with Love:
True Stories from
Peer Counseling,
Revised Edition*

by Joan Sturkie

Clothbound, 270 pages, 6" x 9",
$17.95, ISBN 0-89390-151-2
Paperbound, 270 pages, 6" x 9",
$11.95, ISBN 0-89390-150-4

*Teacher's Guide to
Listening With Love*

by Dr. Alisann Frank,
edited by Joan Sturkie

Paper, $9.95, 64 pages, 5½" x 8½"
ISBN 0-89390-161-X

Listening With Love is a book of issues universal among young
people today. It was created by Joan Sturkie, a former high
school counselor and peer counseling teacher who now serves
as a consultant for school peer helping programs. In this book,
Joan gives stories from real students in actual classes that
relate specific problems and some of the solutions that develop.
Includes a chapter on how to start and maintain a peer helping
program in your school.

Listening With Love can be used as a text for a peer helping
course. The *Teacher's Guide to Listening with Love* will help
you plan lessons based on the text. For each chapter in the
text, this teacher's guide presents an opening lecturette,
questions for post-reading, activity suggestions, and a brief
preview to get ready for the next lesson. The teacher's guide
gives you a way to focus the students on their own feelings
about the issues discussed in the stories in *Listening with Love*.

Order from your local bookseller, or use the order form on the last page.

Discussion Starters for Teens!

*Acting It Out:
74 Short Plays for Starting
Discussions With Teenagers*

by Joan Sturkie and
Marsh Cassady, Ph.D.

Paperbound, $21.95
358 pages, 6" x 9"
ISBN 0-89390-178-4

Getting teenagers to talk about how they're feeling can be
frustrating. *Acting It Out* offers a role-playing approach: Teens
read or act out a short play, then discuss how the characters
deal with the particular issue. The provided questions help
isolate issues and feelings. These dramas address challenging
subjects: abortion, suicide, child abuse, gangs, anorexia, home
life, drugs. Ideal for classes in peer counseling or for any class
or situation in which values discussions are appropriate.

A Quick Reference for Peer Helpers

The Peer Helper's Pocketbook

by Joan Sturkie
& Valerie Gibson

Paperbound, $7.95
74 pages, 4¼" x 7"
ISBN 0-89390-162-8

The Peer Helpers Pocketbook, by peer counseling consultant
Joan Sturkie and peer counselor Valerie Gibson, provides your
peer helpers with a fast, handy reference. This small book for
pocket or purse gives tips, a review of basic skills, and a section
for important referral telephone numbers—for those times
when more help is indicated.

Order from your local bookseller, or use the order form on the last page.

Other Resources for Counseling

*Gem of the First Water:
A Recovery Process for
Troubled Teenagers*

by Ron Phillips

Paperbound, $14.95
229 pages, 5½" x 8½"
Illustrated
ISBN 0-89390-181-4

In this fable for the '90s, an angry boy finds himself
mysteriously transported to the Land of Confusion. There he
confronts his own anger and lies, and through dealing with
them grows into a young man who can take responsibility for
himself. Author Ron Phillips, a storyteller, teacher, and family
therapist, has used this story to enlighten many confused
eleven to fourteen year olds about key issues in their lives.

*Whispers of the Heart:
A Journey Toward
Befriending Yourself*

by Dale R. Olen

Paperbound, $8.95
180 pages, 5½" x 8½"
ISBN 0-89390-100-8

The central message of this book is that behavior arises from
fundamental core energies that are good. The energy to exist,
the energy to act freely, the energy to love. By learning to get
in touch with these energies, you can learn to celebrate your
own goodness, relate more effectively to others, and enter more
fully into your daily life experiences.

Order from your local bookseller, or use order form on last page.

New for School Counselors...

Partners in Healing: Redistributing Power in the Counselor-Client Relationship

by Barbara Friedman, Ph.D.

Paperbound, $14.95
144 pages, 5½" x 8½"
ISBN 0-89390-226-8

Are you looking for a way to empower your student clients, without just telling them the answers to their problems?

By redefining the boundaries between you and your students, you can work *together* in the process of self-discovery and healing. Use this book to learn how to set boundaries—then enjoy the results of a *mutually empowered* counselor-client relationship!

Dr. Barbara Friedman *is a psychologist and writer. She has extensive training in Jungian and Gestalt psychology. A certified chemical dependepncy counselor, she is the director and supervising psychologist at the Walnut Hills Center in Orange Village, Ohio.*

ORDER FORM

LY